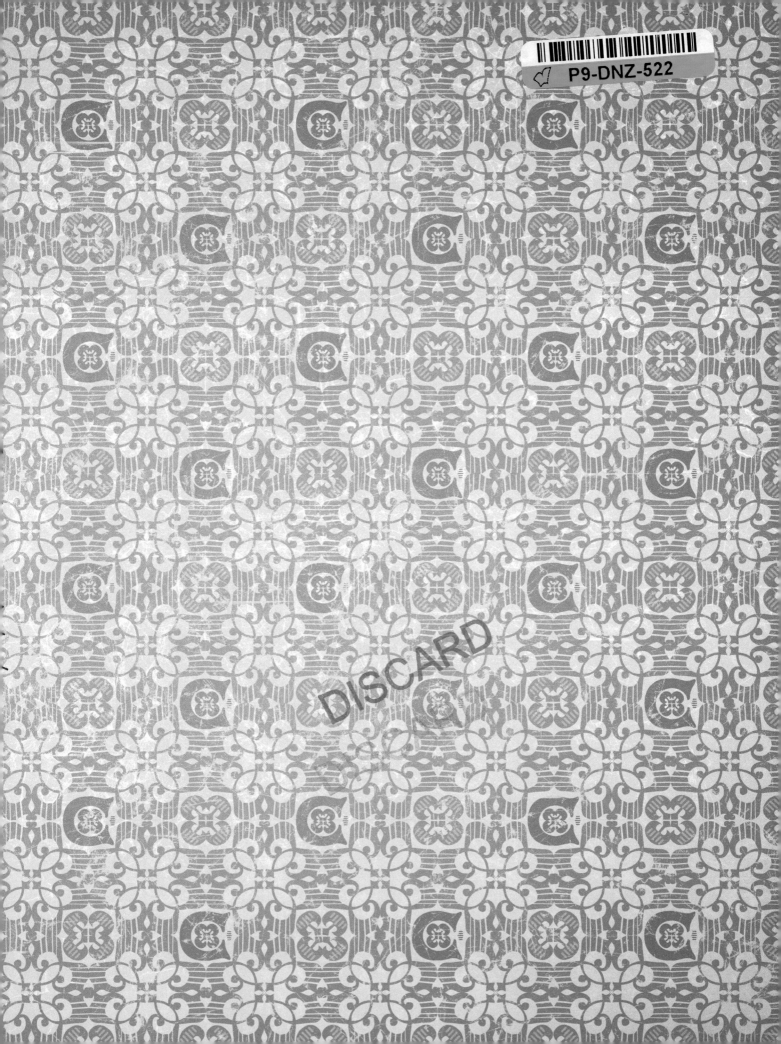

CASH

by the editors of

# ROLLING STONE

* * * * *

foreword by
ROSANNE
**CASH**

* * * * *

edited by
JASON
**FINE**

* * * * *

**CROWN PUBLISHERS**
NEW YORK

EDITOR: Jason Fine
ASSOCIATE EDITOR: Jenny Eliscu
EDITORIAL ASSISTANT: Lauren Gitlin

ART DIRECTOR: Gail Anderson; SpotCo
DESIGNERS: Jessica Disbrow, Sam Eckersley, Bashan Aquart

PHOTOGRAPHY EDITOR: Jodi Peckman
ASSOCIATE PHOTOGRAPHY EDITOR: Amelia Halverson

COPY EDITOR: Allison Xantha Miller
RESEARCH: Andy Gensler

BUSINESS MANAGER: Evelyn Bernal

Published by Crown Publishers, New York, New York.
Member of the Crown Publishing Group, a division of Random House, Inc.
www.crownpublishing.com

CROWN is a trademark and the Crown colophon is a
registered trademark of Random House, Inc.

Portions of this work have been previously published in
*Rolling Stone* magazine and *Cash: The Autobiography*.
Selections from *Cash: The Autobiography* reprinted by permission of
HarperCollins Publishers Inc. Copyright © 1997 by John R. Cash

Printed in the United States of America

Library of Congress Cataloging-in-Publication Data is available upon request.

ISBN 1-4000-5480-X

10 9 8 7 6 5 4 3 2 1

First Edition

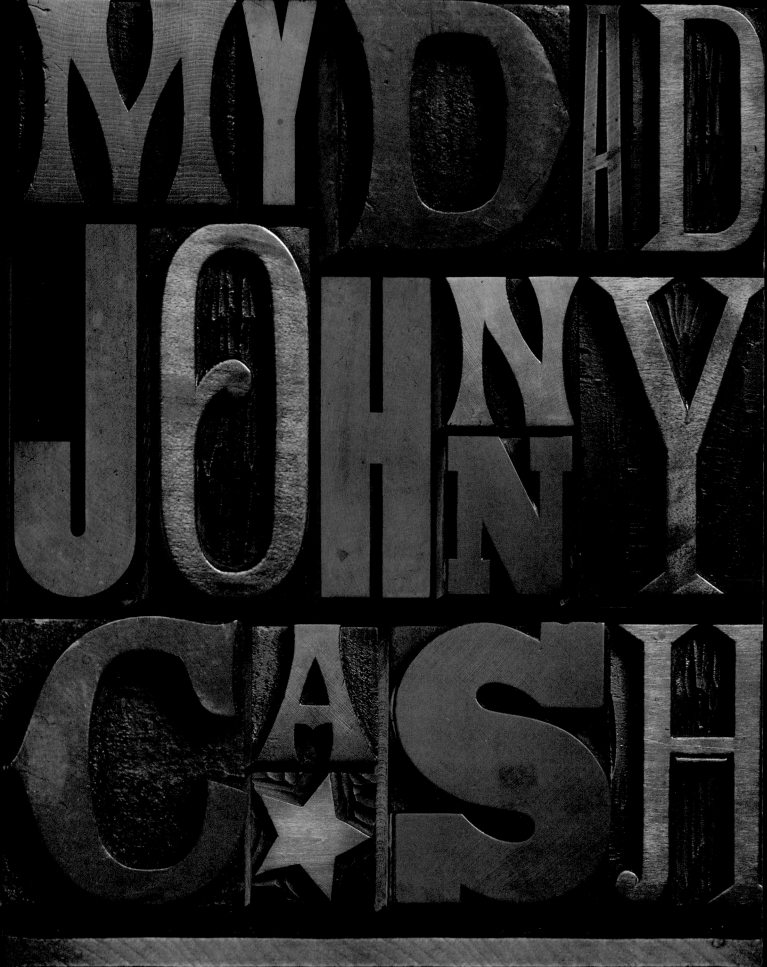

By **ROSANNE CASH**

# The summer I was twelve years old, my father

decided that all of us children should learn to water-ski. Every day we started right after break-fast — me, my three younger sisters, Kathy, Cindy and Tara, and my two stepsisters, Rosey and Carlene — and we loaded up the boat, which was docked at the bottom of the stone steps leading down from the house, and headed out onto Old Hickory Lake.

Dad was serene, focused and relentless. He drove the boat to the center of the lake, tightened our life jackets and sent us each overboard in turn. He waited until we were in position behind the boat, leaning back in the water, clutching the rope, skis sticking straight up, then he gunned the engine. He gunned the engine about a hundred times a day, and some days nobody got up to standing. Most of the time he had a Coke and a bag of peanuts in his hand, and he absentmindedly dropped peanuts in his bottle and swigged it all back. When someone finally got up to standing and skied for a few seconds, he

WITH HIS BABY GIRL *Rosanne, born in 1955. "It was not the scope of his artistry that made him great," she says. "He was already great."*

11

whooped and waved his arm and hollered and congratulated us effusively.

We spent long hours every day on the lake, and by the end of the summer, all of us were skiing. I did pretty well. I learned to drop a ski and do some twists and turns, nothing really fancy, but more fun than I had ever had in my life. I don't remember Dad ever getting up on the skis himself. He just put himself at our service.

My dad brought the same level of focus and patience to everything he did, both work and play. I have a vivid image of him hunched over an old-fashioned hand-cranked ice cream maker, out in the yard at dusk, turning the handle for hours without complaint, and then spooning out to each of us bowls of the most delicious ice cream in the world, stirred with fresh peaches from the orchard. Then he opened up a big bag of fireworks and set them off right in front of us while we lounged on the grassy slope and ate the ice cream. He probably burned his hand ten times a night, but he never said a word about it. All my memories of him have those qualities of silence, patience, love and stoicism: watching him facing thousands of people under a spotlight with his guitar slung across his back, or out in the yard, making ice cream and burning his hand on the fireworks.

My sisters and my brother, John Carter, who was born when I was fifteen, knew two separate but connected beings: Daddy and Johnny Cash. The larger-than-lifeness, the iconic nature and luminous spirit, if they were distilled down to a series of private and precious moments, that is where we found our daddy. It was not the scope of his artistry that made him great; he was already great. In the smallest, most trivial events of daily life, he thought as a great artist, he found the raw center of everything, he zeroed in on the source of love or pain.

Once, when I was a teenager, I was lying on the bed in my room, reading a book on astrology. Dad walked in and asked me what I was reading. I handed him the book and said, "You don't believe in this, do you?" He looked at the book, handed it back to me and said, "No, but I think you should find out everything you can about it." He had tuned right in to the critical instant of opportunity to impress my developing character. And he did it instinctually, without thinking. That one comment became the template on which I later based my entire philosophy of parenting: one of trust, respect and a wide-open mind.

My father's own wide-open mind explored an immense universe of ideas, of sound, beauty, mystery, love, pain and rhythm. He offered that universe to us, his children, as our birthright: to delight in our own treasures and slam up against our own walls, always knowing that his love was close at hand. He never criticized his children, never condescended, never raised his voice or lectured. He offered advice only when we asked for it, and then he would measure his words with kindness and respect. He never adopted a mantle of authority to "teach" us how to avoid or repair our mistakes. Instead, he lived with his own mistakes openly and learned from them with humility and a spiritual rigor.

He was willing to live with the weight of his own pain — his grief over the loss of his brother in childhood, his on-and-off torment with substance abuse and his natural depth of feeling in all realms — without making anyone else pay for it, which, to me, was and is the definition of integrity. It was an incomparable lesson.

Daddy himself was a tremendous energy source, a radiant center of love in our lives. His heart was so expansive and his mind so finely tuned that he could contain both darkness and light, love and trouble, fear and faith, wholeness and shatteredness, old-school and postmodern, the sacred and the silly, God and the Void.

He was a Baptist with the soul of a mystic.

He was a poet who worked in the dirt.

He was an enlightened being who was wracked with the suffering of addiction and grief.

He was real, whole and more alive to the subtleties of this world and the worlds beyond than anyone I have ever known or even heard of.

He was the stuff of dreams, and the living cornerstone of our lives.

And all of who he was, what he felt and thought, how he walked, talked and breathed in every moment of every day, was underscored by the Rhythm. There was a perpetual engine inside his body and soul. When he was onstage, it found full expression, but it was there even in the mundane or sleepy moments, having lunch, watching television, driving a car, staring into space. He hummed, he twitched, he beat out a tempo with his head and hands and toes that seemed to originate in his very cells. He was bound and liberated by rhythm.

Having said all this, there are still no words good enough to tell you who he was, who he still is and the enormity of the empty space he has left in our lives. A friend told me that your parents keep teaching you even after they are gone. My sisters and my brother and I have already found that to be true. He keeps pointing us in the direction of our best selves, the selves we find when we borrow his wide universe of ideas, his endless patience, his vast love and his acceptance of paradox.

Because he understood those paradoxes inside himself so well, he also knew that every day held a choice. The choices became simpler as he grew older: He grew wiser, he saw consequences more readily, he was more willing to let things go. I cannot count the times I heard him say, "Children, you can choose love or hate. I choose love."

There will never be a world without Johnny Cash. His voice, his songs, the image of him with his guitar slung over his back, all that he was and said and sang and strummed is in our collective memory and documented for future generations. However, I am still, and always will be, trying to understand how to live in a world without Daddy. The best way I know is to begin by saying, "Daddy, in my own wide universe of choices, I also choose love. And rhythm."

# EDITOR'S NOTE

VISITED JOHNNY CASH at his home outside Nashville in early November 2002, a little less than a year before he died. The occasion was the release of his album *American Recordings IV: The Man Comes Around*. Cash's health was poor, and the interview did not go well. He had trouble gathering the breath to answer questions, and although he kept trying, after about twenty minutes it seemed best to stop.

I left Cash alone in his small, book-lined office and drove back to my hotel feeling discouraged and worried for his health. A few hours later, as I was getting ready to head for the airport, the phone rang. It was Cash. "I'm real sorry about today," he said. "I have good days and bad days. If it's not too much trouble, maybe you can come out to the house tomorrow morning and we'll try again."

The next morning I arrived early and walked through the sprawling lakeside home to Cash's office, where he spent most of his time. The room was about ten feet by six feet, crowded with books, antique guns, boxes of bullets and rare coins from his collection. He was sitting in the same wooden chair as the day before, wearing the same denim shirt. He looked just as frail, but he clearly felt better – energized, resolute, ready to talk. Cash had set out coffee, sodas and water on his desk, and he had queued up a CD by the Golden Gate Quartet, one of his favorite gospel groups. He sang along, then he asked me to take his guitar off a hook on the wall so he could play some of the gospel songs he was working on for his next record. I can still feel the buzz of sitting three feet away from Johnny Cash as he played a tune he wrote, "Half a Mile a Day": "The road to heaven/Never had a rapid transit plan/It's one way with no changes/Straight through the promised land...."

We talked for about an hour, mostly about music but also about family, drugs, the Bible, gardening and the impending war in Iraq – all topics Cash spoke about with a keen and nuanced intelligence. He said that he and June were on a low-fat, no-salt diet and that these days they enjoyed fruit smoothies for breakfast. Today, though, Cash said he wanted to break the rules and have a breakfast sandwich – his own invention of two fried eggs and crisp bacon on cinnamon toast. After the interview, we sat at the dining room table and each ate two, and then we shared a third.

By the time breakfast was over, I noticed that I no longer saw a sick man sitting across from me. I saw the Johnny Cash you'll read about in this book, the one conjured simply by the rugged, almost mythic sound of his name: a man of imposing authority, great humanity, dignity, suffering and faith. His body may have been failing, but his spirit was strong. He was still, unquestionably, the Man in Black.

When Cash died, on September 12th, 2003, ROLLING STONE published a special issue on his life and music. We were struck by the passionate reflections of so many of his friends and fellow musicians, including Bob Dylan, Bono, Tom Petty, Al Gore and Kris Kristofferson. When we began to put this book together, I was again amazed by how many people were eager to help. I sifted through boxes of photos and letters provided by Cash's children – Rosanne, Kathy, Cindy, Tara and John. I picked out Valentine's notes from Cash to his young daughters and a report card from his junior year in high school (conduct: A; punctuality: D). The photos are intimate and extraordinary: Cash goofing off in the pool; dancing (a rare occurrence) at Rosanne's 1979 wedding; teaching a few of his thirteen grandchildren to fish. ("You have to talk to the worm and apologize for killing it," he liked to tell his pupils.)

When his wife of thirty-five years, June Carter Cash, passed away in May 2003, Cash said there was only one thing he wanted to do: make music. So he went back to the studio ten days later and recorded fifty songs before he said goodbye. From the snap of his Sun singles to the stately grace of those final recordings made alone in a log cabin, Cash's music stood for simple values: dignity, compassion for working people and the conviction that music has the power to make our world a better place. The man may be gone, but his music remains a place where you can find those things, and much more – the darkness he struggled with, the America he believed in and the peace he wished for all of us. —JASON FINE

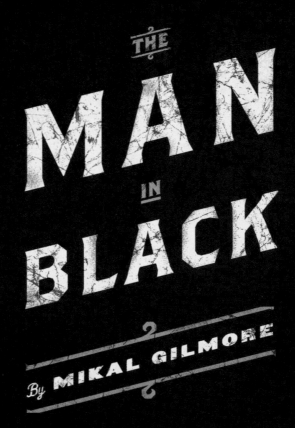

THE

# MAN

IN

# BLACK

By MIKAL GILMORE

# When **JOHNNY CASH** died, on September 12, 2003,

it came as a blow to American music. It wasn't just that we had lost a towering giant of an earlier era — the most influential figure in country music since Hank Williams transformed the heart and soul of the tradition in the 1950s — that made his loss so affecting. Rather, it was that, at age seventy-one, Cash was still a vital contemporary artist. For the last several years he had been making some of the most consistent, daring and probing music by any major contemporary artist, in any genre or

*IN THE STUDIO, 1959. Following his four-year tenure at Sun Records, Cash jumped to Columbia in 1958.*

idiom of popular music. He did this even though he had been brought dangerously low, time and again, by a mysterious illness that altered everything recognizable about him but the intensity of his art and dignity, and his unmistakable, sonorous voice. He continued in those efforts even after the unanticipated death, in May 2003, of the woman he had loved for more than forty years, country and folk singer June Carter Cash. Johnny Cash

kept singing until his end days because singing was his way of living the examined life and of keeping faith with what that life taught him. Keeping faith mattered to him.

Indeed, his first great hit, the 1956 Sun single "I Walk the Line," was a vow — a pledge to stay true to his family, his love, his beliefs and his standards: "I keep a close watch on this heart of mine/I keep my eyes wide open all the time/ I keep the ends out for the tie that binds/Because you're mine, I walk the line." It was a brooding performance, and a brilliant one. The song's

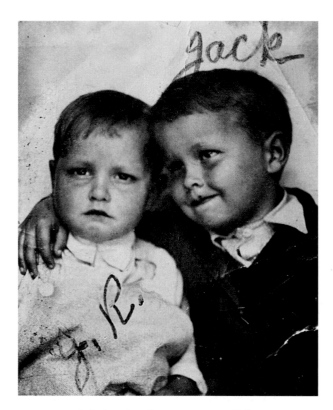

strange, modulating chord sequences — and the mesmerizing way those shifts played out the tricky balance the singer was trying to maintain — were unlike anything else in popular or country music at the time, even in that heyday of unprecedented rock & roll invention. But the song also claimed an impossible ideal for Cash. He was not an unswerving man. In fact, he strayed a lot — into rebellion, into abject addictions, into faithlessness of many sorts. It was the ways Cash fell — not only down but into hard truths — that gave him and his music such uncommon depths, though those depths came at considerable costs.

"Johnny Cash was out of line all his life," Merle Haggard said during the last years of Cash's life. " 'I Walk the Line' was kind of ludicrous for him to sing: 'I walk the line.' He never walked any line.' " Which is true. But Cash was good for one promise he made in that first hit: He kept a close watch on his heart. He had to. After all, he knew what it was capable of.

\* \* \* \* \* \*

OHNNY CASH SOUNDED and looked and moved like a man who had come up through hard times. He was from a people who carried the fear of God in their blood, and who also carried hard-won dreams of a deliverance that their history told them might not always be redeemed in this life. The family traced its lineage back to the family of Caesche, related to early royalty in Scotland; the clan's motto, born through the generations, was "Better times will come." Cash's first American ancestor was a captain who brought pilgrims to the new land, then settled in Massachusetts himself. His descendants eventually migrated to Arkansas, where William Henry Cash became a farmer and a preacher who traveled his circuit with a gun. William's youngest son, Ray, was Johnny Cash's father; William died when Ray was fifteen, and Ray supported his mother until she died a few years later. In 1920, Ray married Carrie Rivers. Carrie had preacher blood in her family as well: Her father, John L. Rivers, was a skilled music teacher and singer; he led the choir in his church, and people would come from miles around to hear his voice. Ray and Carrie settled into cotton farming and had seven children. Johnny Cash was their fourth. He was born in Kingsland, Arkansas, on February 26th, 1932, with no real name. His parents simply called him J.R. Years later, they decided *J* stood for John; they never did figure out what *R* stood for.

By the time Cash was born, the Depression of the 1930s had overcome much of America. Few people were hit as hard as Southern farmers. Cotton growers like his parents, he noted in his second memoir, *Cash: The Autobiography,* had been making meager livings in the best of times, near the bottom of the Southern economy. When the Depression hit, it devastated them. Ray took work where he could, sometimes clearing land and laying track for railroads. When there was no work, he would hop a train to raise money elsewhere. The family's home was next to railroad tracks, and Cash later said one of his first memories was the sight of his father jumping from a moving boxcar and landing in front of the house. That image, and the meanings of that sort of subsistence, stayed with Cash and figured in his music for the rest of his life. The first song he claimed to remember was "I Am Bound for the Promised Land," sung by his mother on a winter night in late 1934, as the family was loaded in a flatbed truck, headed for a new home in the settlement of Dyess, Arkansas. Dyess was an experiment in President Franklin D. Roosevelt's New Deal plan to end the Depression, a limited community where families of farmers chosen by the government formed a cooperative colony as a form of economic recovery. Later, Cash sometimes said, "I grew up under socialism," and in fact these colonies were controversial among some landowners, who saw a place like Dyess as a menace to the ways of Southern agriculture. Still, Dyess succeeded in its early years. The Cashes grew cotton, and every member of the family, from the parents to the youngest, participated in the drudgery of that work.

Carrie taught her children to sing in the fields and in the evening at home as a way of enduring the hard work and as an act of family and faith. On Sundays, the Cashes attended the community's Baptist chapel; though Carrie was a Methodist, she served as the church's pianist. Cash wasn't enamored of church at first. The preacher's shouting, the congregants' writhing and crying — it all terrified him. "I could see no joy in what they were doing," he said. Rather, it was the songs that moved him, and through them he began to find his way to an understanding of the preacher's visions of fear and redemption. He began to use songs as his way to pray, and his mother encouraged him to keep singing; she heard something of her own family in his voice, she told him. Later, Carrie took on extra work doing laundry to buy her son voice lessons. But when Cash's teacher heard him sing Hank Williams' "Long Gone Lonesome Blues," she told him, "Don't ever take voice lessons again. Don't let me or anyone else change the way you sing." Cash's father, though, was hardly as encouraging. "You're wasting your time," Ray told his son. "You'll never do any good as long as you've got that music on the mind."

In interviews throughout most of his career, and in his first autobiography, *Man in Black*, Cash spoke of his father in ideal terms as a good man and a staunch family head. Sometimes, though, Cash told his own children different accounts, and in his 1997 autobiography, he shared a much more blunt perspective with his collaborator, journalist and historian Patrick Carr. His father, Cash said, never encouraged his son or expressed pride in him until after Cash was already successful at recording. "He never once told me he loved me," Cash said, "and he never had a loving hand to lay on any of us children." Sometimes, Ray would come home drunk and rage at his wife. One time he intended to beat her, but Cash's older brother Jack intervened. And then, when Cash was five, his father killed his young son's dog. There were too many dogs around, Ray said, and besides, the family had another

one, also named Ray, that he preferred. "I thought my world had ended that morning," Cash wrote later, "that nothing was safe, that life wasn't safe. It was a frightening thing, and it took me a long time to get over it. It was a cut that went deep and stayed there."

*Stationed in Germany in the Air Force, Cash intercepted Soviet transmissions and learned to drink beer.*

As a result of his father's cruelty, Cash turned ever closer to his older brother Jack, who was more nurturing. Jack was planning to be a minister, and it was his devotion to his younger brother's spiritual well-being that led Cash to declare himself a Christian at a young age. Many nights, Cash said, he and his brother would stay up late, Jack studying the Bible and Cash listening to the family's mail-order Sears & Roebuck radio, catching channels from New Orleans, Chicago, Fort Worth and other faraway places. Cash found a lot of music he liked: the honky-tonk and country balladeering of Hank Williams, Roy Acuff, Eddy Arnold and Ernest Tubb; the gospel blues of Sister Rosetta Tharpe and the bluegrass gospel of the Louvin Brothers; and the swinging pop music of Bing Crosby and the Andrews Sisters. But what compelled him the most was the sound coming from the Grand Ole Opry in Nashville and the haunting songs of country's most important early voices, the Carter Family and Jimmie Rogers, both of whom had helped expand and popularize Appalachian and Southern folk traditions. "Nothing in the world was as

THE CARTER FAMILY:
*June, Anita and Helen*
*(from left) and their*
*mother, Maybelle (seated).*
*Cash first saw the group at*
*the Grand Ole Opry in 1950.*

important to me as hearing those songs on the radio," Cash wrote in *Man in Black.* "The music carried me up above the mud, the work and the hot sun." He would pull his ear closer to the radio, trying to comprehend the stories and lives and places these voices sang about, until his father yelled, "Turn that radio off! You're wasting your time listening to them old records."

One afternoon when he was twelve, Cash was walking home from fishing when his father and the church pastor drove up and told him to drop his pole and get in the car. Cash knew from his father's manner that it was serious. Jack, they told him, was cutting wood on a table saw at the agricultural shop where he had been earning a few extra dollars for the family. He had fallen across the blade; he was cut through his ribs and stomach, down to his groin. Jack was unconscious when Cash reached the hospital, but came around a few days later — lively, laughing, talking about the future. But he soon lapsed, and three days later the family stood by his bedside as he called to his mother in a delirium, describing the beautiful angels he was seeing. Then he died. Cash's eldest daughter, singer Rosanne Cash, later said of her father, "He can't be read or understood out of the context of losing his brother. After that, he was driven by his grief." Cash himself said, "There's no way around grief and loss . . . sooner or later you just have to go into it. . . . The world you find there will never be the same as the world you left."

The death of his brother, the heartlessness of his father, the confinement he felt in Dyess – it all began to breed restlessness in Cash, and an itch for rebellion. He took to walking down the dark night roads around Dyess, humming songs to himself, thinking about those voices he'd heard on the radio and their descriptions of sadness, which were also a means to tales of a hard-earned hope. "The long walk home at night was scary," he wrote in the liner notes to his album *American Recordings*. "It was pitch dark on the gravel road, or if the moon was shining, the shadows were even scarier. . . . But I sang all the way home. . . . I sang through the dark, and I decided that that kind of music was going to be my magic to take me through all the dark places."

* * * * * *

URING HIS YEARS at Dyess High School in the late 1940s, Cash had his first formative glimpses of a musical life. When he was eighteen, his senior class took a field trip to the Grand Ole Opry. That night he got to see the second-generation lineup of his favorite vocal group, the Carter Family, led by original member Mother Maybelle, singing now with her three daughters. Cash particularly liked the youngest Carter, June. She was a funny and resourceful comedian, she had a wail that was both plaintive and impish, and she was pretty. Another time, while listening to the *High Noon Roundup* – a popular country show from Memphis – Cash heard that the Louvin Brothers, his favorite country duo, would be appearing at the Dyess High School auditorium. He was at the school hours early that night and got a chance to speak with Charlie Louvin. (More to the point, Charlie asked the teenager where the bathroom was.) During the show, the Louvins sang a song at Cash's request, "The Kneeling Drunkard's Plea," written by June Carter. Cash later said that the Louvins' show was a turning point for him. "Nobody would believe what I wanted to say . . . : 'I'll be up there someday. That's what I'm gonna be.' I had no doubt."

After graduating from high school, Cash hitchhiked north to Pontiac, Michigan, to take a factory job at an automobile construction plant. He hated the job, he hated the crowded housing, and he hated the manners of the men he worked with, who swore, drank and chased women in ways that ran against his Southern religious ethic. A few weeks later, he hitchhiked back home, but there was no future there, even if he'd wanted to stay in farming. The land was losing its yield, and in time, the rest of Cash's family – like so many others in the fading community – would pack up and leave Dyess, about the time they finished paying the government back for their homes. With no other immediate options, Cash enlisted in the United States Air Force for four years, as the Korean War was underway and the Cold War was hitting its stride. He was stationed at Landsberg, Germany, where he found that he had a knack for quickly decrypting Morse code and intercepting Soviet radio transmissions. In fact, it was Cash who located the signal of the first Soviet jet bomber on its maiden flight from Moscow, and he was also the first Westerner to decipher the news that the Soviet leader Joseph Stalin had died on March 5th, 1953, of a brain hemorrhage.

His German tour of duty also proved a portent of Cash's future in some important ways. At first, he did a good job of living by his back-home standards; he stayed away from the rowdier men and didn't join them on their three-day drunks. Instead, he formed a guitar and string band, the Landsberg Barbarians, with a few other enlisted men. They stuck around the barracks, playing country and gospel songs – like "The Wild Side of Life" and "The Great Speckled Bird" – and Cash became more serious about learning guitar, concentrating on playing rhythm with his thumb, which later became his signature style. It wasn't long, however, before Cash learned those things that most other enlisted men learned: "how to cuss, how to look for women, how to drink and fight." It started off with beer. Everybody in Germany drank it; it seemed harmless enough. Then some German cognac; he liked that. Then he stopped attending church services at the base chapel and stopped writing to his family. By his third year in Germany, he was joining the other men on their three-day benders. He got into fights, and into trouble with local police. He picked up a crooked nose from a fight with a paratrooper (and also acquired a deep scar on his cheek from a drunken German doctor searching for a cyst). One time, Cash knocked out two security guards when they tried to stop him while he was on his way to sell cigarettes on the local black market. On another occasion, he was sitting at a typewriter, working, when he started crying and threw his typewriter out the window. An officer sent him to the dispensary to take some aspirin.

The problem, he said later, was that he was feeling wayward from his life and values. But at the same time, he was learning that he had a capacity for thoughts and impulses that fascinated him, and also scared him. He started writing songs seriously while in Germany, and remarkably enough, one of his earliest compositions was "Folsom Prison Blues." He wrote the song after watching a film about the reality of life at Folsom Prison, one of the oldest penitentiaries in California. He decided, he said in *Cash*, to write from the perspective of an unremorseful killer: "[The] line . . . that still gets the biggest rise out of my audiences . . . – 'I shot a man in Reno just to watch him die' – is imaginative, not autobiographical. I sat with my pen in my hand, trying to think of the worst reason a person could have for killing another person, and that's what came to mind. It did come to mind quite easily, though." Perhaps Cash was starting to recognize some of the dark notions in his own heart and where those urges might land him.

WITH FIRST WIFE *Vivian Liberto, the mother of Cash's four daughters, in 1958. He wrote "I Walk the Line" to prove his loyalty to her.*

\* \* \* \* \* \*

JUST PRIOR TO shipping out to Germany, Cash was skating at a roller rink in San Antonio, Texas, when he crashed into an attractive dark-haired woman named Vivian Liberto. The two wrote each other almost daily, carrying on a romance by mail while Cash was in the Air Force. When he arrived back in the States in July 1954, he said, the couple knew two things: They were going to marry, and he would be a singer. At first, Cash's wife supported his ambition. She even agreed to move to Memphis – in part so that Cash could be close to his older brother Roy, who worked at the Automobile Sales Company, but also because Memphis was then the most vital music city in the South. It had long been an important blues town and for a time was a Western swing center. By the mid-1950s, when Cash and Vivian moved there, the city was undergoing waves

of inspired creativity that would have far-reaching and world-changing effects. Cash took a job as a door-to-door salesman, peddling home appliances, but his heart wasn't in it. Sometimes he seemed so distracted and impertinent to customers that they shut the door on him or threatened to call the police. As often as not, he'd just stay in his car, listening to the rhythm & blues and country and gospel stations that characterized Memphis in those years. Cash also spent a lot of time in black neighborhoods, listening to spirituals and blues and picking up guitar tips, and he spent time and money at the Home of the Blues — a superb record store where he discovered Alan Lomax's influential folk and blues collections.

By the time Cash had moved to Memphis, producer Sam Phillips and his label, Sun Records, were already important forces in the local music scene. Phillips had been producing a stunning array of black blues and R&B singers, including Howlin' Wolf, Junior Parker, B.B. King, Bobby "Blue" Bland, Little Milton and Rufus Thomas, but he had dreamed for some time of finding a white singer who could carry urban blues over to a larger pop audience with uncompromised spirit and authority. Phillips fulfilled that dream, of course, in the nineteen-year-old prodigy Elvis Presley, who helped fuse blues and country into an innovative blend called rockabilly, and who would spearhead the national explosion of rock & roll. Cash and Vivian had seen Presley at one of his first flatbed truck performances in Memphis and struck up a friendly acquaintance with him. Cash, though, already knew that his own strength was with more somber songs, backed by strong but meditative rhythms. He thought Phillips might be interested in the spare, rhythmic kind of gospel he had been working up. For better and worse, he was wrong.

There is a legend — almost certainly apocryphal — that when Phillips first heard Cash's aspiration to sing gospel, he said, "Go back home and sin, and then come back with something I can sell." What Phillips actually told Cash was that while he liked gospel, he could never sell enough of it to justify its production and promotion costs — and besides, he was too busy with Presley to take on anything new. Cash tried a couple of other approaches that also met with rejection, and so one morning he sat down on the front stoop of Sun Records, holding his guitar, waiting for Phillips. He caught the producer in a good mood that day. Phillips said, "You don't give up, do you?" Minutes later Cash was inside the Sun studio, regaling the producer with his versions of Jimmie Rodgers, Carter Family and Hank Snow songs. What Phillips noticed immediately — what he couldn't miss, he said later — was Cash's voice: It was low, sepulchral and full of loneliness in a way that Phillips had never heard before from a pop or country singer. Phillips knew he wanted that voice — he could do something with it if it was put together with the right song and arrangement. He asked Cash to sing something original. Cash sang what he regarded as his best song at the time, "Belshazzar," but even though it was an upbeat kicker, it was still a spiritual. "What else do you have?" Phillips asked. Cash reluctantly played "Hey Porter," an anthem to the South that he had written in Germany but didn't like. Phillips decided that was the one. He told Cash to come back the next day with a band and they would record that song.

Cash had been playing with some like-minded musicians — bassist Marshall Grant and guitarists Luther Perkins and A.W. "Red" Kernodle — whom he met through his brother Roy at the Automobile Sales Company. Roy himself had been in a 1940s string band called the Dixie Rhythm Ramblers back in Arkansas; when the band's other members were killed in World War II, Roy lost interest in a musical career, but he had always encouraged his younger brother. Cash called Grant, Perkins and Kernodle the Tennessee Three, and they started playing gospel and country at church socials and on Memphis radio, to good responses. That next day, though, when Cash brought the trio to Sun, he felt chagrined about their abilities — he saw them all as basic players. Kernodle, who was playing steel guitar on the session, got so nervous that he quit on the spot, and the Tennessee Three became the Tennessee Two. Since the band had no drummer, Cash and Phillips threaded a piece of paper between the strings of his guitar and its fret board, and Cash played the instrument high on its neck for a strong rhythmic effect. Phillips added some slap-back echo to heighten the band's dynamics. At the end of the day, the producer told Cash he was going to put out their recording of "Hey Porter" as a single, but first they needed another song for the flip side. Phillips wanted a weeper as a contrast. Cash came back the next day with "Cry, Cry, Cry"; it was up-tempo and a little mean-spirited, but it sounded good alongside "Hey Porter." Phillips issued the single in June 1955. It went to Number

One on the Memphis country charts and peaked at Number Fourteen on *Billboard*'s national country charts.

In their first few Sun sessions, Johnny Cash and the Tennessee Two – aided by Sam Phillips' brilliant instincts – created what became Cash's core style for more or less the rest of his life. It was a steady rhythmic sound with spare instrumentation, often called the *boom-chicka-boom* sound for its simple picking patterns and the cadence of its backbeat. (In 1960, Cash added session drummer W.S. "Fluke" Holland to the touring lineup, and his band was once more the Tennessee Three.) Over the years, many critics – including Cash himself – have wondered how lasting greatness came from such limited accompaniment. In *Cash*, the singer noted that Grant and Perkins often restricted the range of material he could perform – and yet the truth is that those limitations were an indispensable element in helping him to invent the power and durability of his best 1950s and 1960s recordings. The spare music framed the isolation in Cash's voice – a voice that, even at age twenty-three, conveyed a sense of haunted experience and regret with rare credibility. It would have been a mistake to allow any ornamentation or flourish to distract the listener from the presence of that voice and the stories it was telling. In time, Cash's straightforward approach would transform country music as surely and as radically as Presley's Sun records had altered popular music. For several years and in various hurtful ways, much of the country world would not forgive Cash for his originality.

* * * * * *

N AUGUST 1955, Cash played the first big show of his career, opening for Elvis Presley. Cash later traced the roots of his marriage's dissolution to that concert. Vivian saw the passionate reactions that Presley was now getting from young women, and she realized that her husband might soon meet with something similar. She took a less supportive view of his music career. Later, to allay his wife's concerns – and likely his own as well – Cash started writing a song called "Because You're Mine." He'd been carrying the tune for it ever since he was in Germany, when an accidentally twisted tape of some music he recorded with the Landsberg Barbarians resulted in the sound of a chord progression played backward, making for an unusual evocative sound. One night, he was playing his new song for guitarist Carl Perkins, who had joined the Sun

fold around the same time as Cash. "I keep a close watch on this heart of mine," Cash sang. "Because you're mine, I walk the line." Cash asked Perkins what he thought. "Y'know, 'I Walk the Line' would be a better title," Perkins said. Cash recorded the song as a declaration of his fidelity and of the ideal man he wanted to be, and yet when it went on to enjoy massive success, it only took him further from his wife and his new daughter, Rosanne.

As it turned out, Cash was trying to walk more than one line at that point. Was it possible, he wondered, to maintain a Christian life in the popular music world while playing in honky-tonks where he found himself drinking more, as he watched men chase women who weren't their wives? Could he withstand those temptations himself? When Jerry Lee Lewis came to Sun a while later, he had some of the same questions Cash had, except Lewis – who had just left Bible school – already *knew* the answer. "I'm out here doing what God don't want me to do, and I'm leading the people to hell!" he'd tell Cash. There was no way a Christian life could be reconciled with a rock & roll or honky-tonk life, Lewis insisted. Cash found himself growing weary of the sermons. Because of his touring schedule, he was now missing church regularly. That bothered him, but it couldn't be helped. Besides, he liked the excitement of playing live shows night after night. Walking the line was becoming something a bit different for him: It was now a matter of being able to stay the course for what his music and touring life were demanding of him.

In 1955, Sam Phillips sold Elvis Presley's contract to RCA Records for $35,000. He then took the money and invested it into promoting "I Walk the Line" – which turned out to be Cash's biggest hit for Sun, climbing to Number One on *Billboard*'s country charts. Despite that success, though, Cash had doubts about his future with Sun. When a trailblazing Columbia Records producer, Don Law (who had documented the music of Robert Johnson and Bob Wills and had worked with Marty Robbins and Lefty Frizzell), approached Cash after a *Town Hall Party* TV appearance in Los Angeles and asked him if he was interested in changing labels after his Sun contract ended, Cash was immediately curious. He wanted to know if Columbia would let him record an album of spirituals – an ambition that Phillips had steadily resisted. Law said yes, that would be no problem. Cash went on to tell the producer about some other,

more ambitious projects he had in mind – concept albums he knew would be impossible given Sun's limited resources – and Law was intrigued. Cash signed an option with Columbia right away. When Phillips caught wind of the deal, he confronted Cash, and Cash lied: He'd signed no option, he said. Phillips was deeply hurt, and Cash must have realized that in deceiving Phillips he was acting out of accord with his own ethics.

At the same time, Cash didn't feel Phillips had been fair with him: Sun wouldn't let him record much of the material that he wanted to record and had started to saddle him with unsuitable pop arrangements. Phillips also wouldn't pay his artists the standard industry royalty rate. But one

of his main grievances, Cash said later, came down to what he perceived as a slight. "[Phillips] never gave me a Cadillac," he wrote in *Cash*. "He gave Carl Perkins one when Carl sold a million copies of 'Blue Suede Shoes,' but I never got one when 'I Walk the Line' became such a huge hit. . . . I still think I should have that Cadillac." Cash and Phillips later mended their friendship; they had too much respect for each other's creativity and historical standing to bear grudges.

Cash moved to Columbia in 1958, and at the same time moved his family – Vivian and daughters Rosanne, Kathy and Cindy – to Los Angeles, to a San Fernando Valley home he purchased from late-night TV host Johnny Carson. Cash was now free to record the music he had long envisioned – including the spirituals that had been his original inspiration for pursuing Sun. But by the time he settled into the recording sessions for *Hymns by Johnny Cash*, he was already on his way down a course that would place both his soul and his life at risk.

✳ ✳ ✳ ✳ ✳ ✳

OHNNY CASH STARTED his Columbia years in terrific form. His first album with Don Law, *The Fabulous Johnny Cash*, showcased a confident and original stylist with an unusually adept feel for mixing country, folk and pop sensibilities. His second single for his new label, "Don't Take Your Guns to Town," was a sparse and riveting portrait of pointless death in the fatalistic American West; its start-and-stop tempo, and the way it created mounting suspense from subtle shifts in tone and rhythm, sounds as fresh and effective today as it did in 1958. The single's flip side, "I Still Miss Someone," was probably the loveliest – and most enduring – song of romantic despair that he would ever write. There was no question: Johnny Cash had fully arrived as a young artist with uncommon new visions for old forms, and with talent to burn.

But as Cash's creativity soared, problems were already setting in. In fact, they had started before the end of his Sun career. Though he denied it through much of his life, Cash had a depressive nature. The years of hardship in Arkansas, as well as the pain he felt over his father's hardness and his brother's death, left him brooding, tense and wary. More immediately, the increasing strain in his marriage and the exhaustion from touring were taking a toll. He had gone rather quickly from struggling ambition to fame, and there were drawbacks to such a blazing transition. The elation he felt onstage, singing his music and seeing its effect on an audience, proved tremendous, but the downturns that came afterward grew unbearable. Writing about Cash in 1974 in *The Great American Popular Singers*, critic Henry Pleasants said, "It seems almost to be a curse . . . that life begins, day after day and night after night, when the curtain goes up and is suspended when it comes down. . . . It was the occasional night off that was regularly and predictably his undoing." One night in 1957, Cash thought he found a remedy for his fatigue and dejection. He was on a tour with Faron Young, Ferlin Husky and several other Grand Ole Opry artists, and he had become friendly with musician Gordon Terry, from Young's band. During an all-night drive, Terry thought that Luther Perkins, who was

driving one of the cars, might be getting sleepy and, according to Cash, offered Perkins a white pill to stay awake. Cash asked what the pill was. Terry said it was "Bennies" – a common term for Benzedrine, Dexedrine and other amphetamines that were popular and readily available at the time. Cash wanted to know if the pills would hurt him. "They've never hurt me," Terry reportedly said. "Here, have one." By the next night, Cash still hadn't slept, so he took another pill before going onstage. He didn't like the comedown from amphetamines – he felt even more tired and depressed – but he liked how he felt when the pills took him up. He thought they enhanced his performing ability, he wrote in *Man in Black*: "My energy was multiplied, my timing was superb, I enjoyed every song in every concert and could perform with a driving, relentless intensity. They made me think faster and talk more." He later told Christopher Wren – the author of an early Cash biography, *Winners Got Scars Too* – that as much as anything, he was perhaps looking for a spiritual satisfaction in drugs.

By the early 1960s, Cash was fully hooked on amphetamines, and he had started mixing them with alcohol and barbiturates so that he could ease off the speedy drugs into sleep. The pills were also affecting his live performances in adverse ways. His timing wasn't as sharp as he had felt before, and after days of taking speed, Cash's voice would turn dry and he would develop laryngitis. Other times, his manner was simply inexplicable. All those problems combined in May 1962, when Cash finally received a chance to bring his music to Carnegie Hall. When he arrived in New York after days on speed, his nerves were shot, and so was his judgment. Cash had an obsession at the time with the music and fate of Jimmie Rodgers, who was called the "Singing Brakeman" because he worked on the rails from his childhood through his early career; his ill health and early death from tuberculosis traced back to the working conditions of those years. That night at Carnegie, Cash strolled onstage dressed in Rodgers' brakeman outfit (he'd obtained it from Rodgers' widow) and carrying Rodgers' railway lamp; he intended to surprise the audience by singing only Jimmie Rodgers songs. The audience, though, didn't understand what Cash was doing, nor did a mystified Don Law, who had planned on recording the show for an already announced live album. The audience yelled instead for "Folsom Prison Blues," and when Cash tried to sing the song, he found he'd lost his voice. He croaked his way through the show, but the night was a debacle.

Yet despite what the drugs were doing to him – maybe even because of what they were doing to him – Cash made some of his most daring and groundbreaking recordings in these years, in an unprecedented series of ambitious folk and country concept albums that included *Songs of Our Soil* (1959), *Ride This Train* (1960), *Blood Sweat and Tears* (1963), *Bitter Tears: Ballads of the American Indian* (1964), *Orange Blossom Special* (1965) and *The Ballads of the True West* (1965). These were works that spoke about the hidden truths, as opposed to the received myths, in American history. The albums also spoke to and about a remarkably diverse range of people, including the poor and the violent, exploited laborers and Native Americans, and jingoists and the dispossessed. In some ways, the series owed something to the 1960s folk resurgence that was then burgeoning on numerous U.S. college campuses and in New York's Greenwich Village, and was having an increasingly liberal-minded effect on American politics. Cash had always heeded folk music – he understood that the Carters and Jimmie Rodgers had emerged from its traditions – and in the early 1960s he formed friendships and alliances with some of the movement's key postwar figures, including Ramblin' Jack Elliott, Pete Seeger and Peter LaFarge (a Hopi Indian who was an exceptional and fearless songwriter). In particular, Cash was smitten with the young Minnesota-born singer and songwriter Bob Dylan, whom he regarded as the best hillbilly singer and most original songsmith he had ever heard. While working a series of clubs in downtown Las Vegas, Cash would stay up through the late hours to the dawn, playing *The Freewheelin' Bob Dylan* and *The Times They Are a-Changin'*. He could hear that Dylan was trying to break new ground and create new freedoms, just as Cash had been attempting in his own music.

Cash's most controversial (and probably best) album in this period was *Bitter Tears*, his spirited and angry essay about the suffering, betrayals, violence and indifference visited upon American Indians. LaFarge (who had drug problems of his own during this time and would shortly die from them) helped Cash with his research for the album and wrote five of the collection's songs, including the album's single, "The Ballad of Ira Hayes": the story of a Pima Indian who was among the U.S. Marine heroes who raised the flag after the bloody World War II battle of Iwo Jima. Hayes later died of neglect and alcoholism, drowning in a two-inch ditch of water. Country radio wouldn't touch the song, which Cash regarded as one of his best recordings. Cash responded with a full-page open-letter ad in *Billboard*, in which he wrote, "D.J.'s – station managers – owners, etc., where are your *guts*?... 'Ballad of Ira Hayes' *is* strong medicine. So is Rochester – Harlem – Birmingham and VietNam.... I had to fight back when I realized that so many stations are afraid of 'Ira Hayes.' " Some Nashville forces were livid. The editor of one magazine, in a subsequent open letter, wrote, "You and your crowd are just too intelligent to associate with plain country folks, country artists and country deejays," and he demanded that Cash resign from the Country Music Association. Country music stations still ignored "Ira Hayes," but it hardly mattered. The song went on to become one of Cash's most successful singles of the mid-1960s.

In 1961, June Carter – the singer Cash had seen years before with the Carter Family – joined Johnny Cash's stage show. Cash had first met her backstage at the Opry, in 1956. He walked over to her and introduced himself. "I know who you are," she said. Years earlier, Carter had toured with Elvis Presley and had a close relationship with him. Sometimes Presley would play Johnny Cash's music for her. He was enamored of the singing, and told Carter that Cash was going to be a big star. That night at the Opry, Cash took her by the hand and said, "I've always wanted to meet you. You and I are going to get married someday." Carter said, "I can't wait." Both were already married – she to country singer Carl Smith, with whom she had a daughter, Carlene. After her marriage with Smith ended, Carter married Rip Nix and had a second daughter, Rosey (who died shortly after Cash's death in 2003).

In the meantime, Cash's drug intake was starting to wear him down – and he responded by taking even greater quantities and by acting wilder and wilder. He began carrying guns and firing them off for little or no reason (he got thrown out of a hotel in Australia when he and Sammy Davis Jr. staged a fast-draw duel in the lobby, firing off blanks and sending other guests fleeing). He even carted a cannon around and occasionally fired it off in his dressing room. He chopped through locked doors in hotels with a hatchet just to wake his band members. Sometimes, after a night of pills and booze, he would piss on the radiator in his

hotel room, creating an unbelievable smell when it came on. Other
nights, he sawed the legs off the
room's furniture, so that "small
people" might have a place to sit. He
dumped a huge load of horse
manure in one hotel lobby. He also wrecked almost every
car he owned, and was lucky to walk away alive from some of
the smashups. His most destructive act in that time, though,
wasn't committed under the influence of drugs, but it was
a product of the neglect and contempt that his drug use was
fostering in him. He was driving a camper, which he knew
had a cracked bearing, in the Los Padres National Wildlife
Refugee, near Ventura, California, when oil dripped from
the bearing onto the sun-hot grass and sparked a fire. A
wind stirred up and the blaze went out of control. Before
emergency crews subdued it, the fire had destroyed three
mountains of forestry in the refuge area and drove out almost
all of the fifty-three protected wild condors living in the area.
The government filed suit, and Cash went into the deposi-
tions high on amphetamines. When an attorney asked him if
he felt bad about what he had done, Cash replied, "Well, I feel
pretty good right now." When he was asked if he felt bad
about driving the condors from their refuge, Cash said, "I
don't give a damn about your yellow buzzards. Why should
I care?" Cash maintained that he was the only U.S. citizen the
government ever successfully sued for setting fire to a
national forest, and he paid $125,000 in damages.

Cash did care, though, about what happened to him at the
Grand Ole Opry in 1965. He went onstage, his nerves raw
from drugs and booze, and when he attempted to take his
microphone from its stand, it wouldn't come loose. "Such
a minor complication in my mental state," he wrote in *Man
in Black*, "was enough to make me explode in a fit of anger.
I took the mike stand, threw it down, then dragged it along
the edge of the stage, popping fifty or sixty headlights. The
broken glass shattered all over the stage and into the audience." He stopped the show and left the stage. The Grand
Ole Opry manager met him at the stage's side and said,
"You don't have to come back anymore. We can't use you."

When Cash left the Opry that night, he was angry, hurt and
humiliated. He was crying while driving. There was a thun-
derstorm, and he ran into a utility pole, breaking his nose.
He ended up in the hospital, where he was given morphine.

The new Cadillac he had been driving was totaled, and the
woman who owned it was June Carter. June was mad as hell
at Cash. So was her husband, Rip Nix, the policeman who
investigated the accident.

* * * * * *

UNE CARTER had developed complicated and troubled feelings about Cash. For one thing, she had
fallen in love with him, and long before either of
them would leave the people they were married to,
Cash and Carter's love affair was more or less an
open secret in the country music world. Carter had known
Hank Williams – she was the godmother of Hank Williams
Jr. – and she didn't want to see Cash wind up the same way
as Williams did, a brilliant artist who destroyed himself
young. The combination of their love and Cash's self-
destructiveness made for a volatile relationship. Carter
interceded at every point she could, sometimes telling
doctors she found backstage not to write him prescriptions. She also learned the places he would hide his drugs
and then uncover and destroy the pills. She and Cash would
get into arguments, and he would throw her possessions
and say horrible, hurtful things to her. One time he told
her, "If you weren't a woman, I'd break your neck." She
shot back, "You'd miss me." Years later, in the liner notes
for Johnny's *Love, God, Murder* collection, Carter said of
their early relationship, "I knew that from first looking at
him that his hurt was as great as mine, and from the depths
of my despair I stepped up to feel the fire and there is no
way to be in that kind of hell, no way to extinguish a flame
that burns, burns, burns." Thoughts like these during an
all-night aimless drive, June said, inspired her to write
"Ring of Fire." When Cash first heard the song, he knew it
was about their love, but he didn't say as much. He did tell
her, though, that he'd had a dream about the song. In the
dream, he heard "Ring of Fire" played by Mexican horns,
and he was singing along with it. After he realized that
dream in 1963, the song dominated *Billboard*'s country
charts for seven weeks, rising to Number One.

* * * * * *

IVIAN TRIED to pull Cash back into their family
in California and to persuade him to stop taking
uppers and downers. Cash would spend the
occasional few hours, maybe a day, at home with his wife
and children, but then he was off – on tour or looking for

more drugs. Once or twice, he admitted later, he even robbed pharmacies. During a stopover in El Paso in 1965, Cash decided to cross the border to Juarez, Mexico. He had heard that he could readily acquire large quantities of drugs there, and with the help of a taxi driver, he came back to the U.S. with bags of pills. As he sat in his plane on the airstrip in El Paso, police officers arrested him. They found 688 Dexedrines and 475 capsules of Equanil (an anti-anxiety agent) stuffed inside a cheap Mexican guitar and the lining of his suitcase, and arrested Cash for illegally obtaining amphetamines and barbiturates. Speaking to a reporter after the arrest, Cash said, "I don't pretend to be anything I'm not. . . . I am guilty of as many sins as the average person, but I don't say that I am guilty of any more than the average person. I may have a few different ones, but certainly no more."

Vivian came to El Paso to stand by Cash's side when he was released from jail. Later, some white supremacists saw a photo of her and didn't like what they judged to be her dark skin. The Ku Klux Klan started picketing Cash's shows, branding him a degenerate who had mongrel children. ("If there's a mongrel in the crowd, it's me," Cash fired back at the Klan, "because I'm Irish and one quarter Cherokee" — though if in fact there was any Cherokee blood in Cash, it was considerably less than that.) When the drug possession case went to trial, Cash received a thirty-day suspended sentence and a fine of $1,000. Don Law paid it for him.

In October 1967, Cash finally hit his end. He had lost an alarming amount of weight, and no amount of drugs could any longer calm his jitters or fears. If he had once thought he could find a spiritual state in drugs, that thought was long gone. He had cut himself off from God, he felt, and in some ways that estrangement hurt even more than being separated from his wife and four daughters. He decided to crawl into Nickajack Cave on the Tennessee River and let himself die there. He crawled for hours, until his flashlight gave out, and he lay down, feeling empty of everything good that had ever been inside him. But an unexpected feeling came over him, he later said. He realized that he couldn't die there, and that he would no longer continue his descent into drugs and madness. When he emerged from the cave, June Carter was standing there, and so was his mother. Johnny Cash would go through withdrawal in the next month, and he would recommit himself to his life and his music and his faith, with more devotion and insight than

before. Vivian granted him the divorce he sought, and on March 1st, 1968, after several months clean and sober, he married June Carter. The couple settled into Cash's sprawling, eccentric, countrified mansion in Hendersonville, twenty miles north of Nashville. Johnny Cash's most famous moment in music lay just ahead of him, and when he arrived at that moment, he brought with him everything he had learned from the lower depths about how sometimes people's lives went wrong and they found themselves in dark places, cut off from hope and forgiveness.

\* \* \* \* \* \*

N THE LATE 1960s, Don Law — who had overseen most of Cash's brilliant earlier Columbia work and had stood by the singer despite his failings — resigned from Columbia, and Cash hooked up with another maverick mind, Bob Johnston. Johnston had worked with Marty Robbins and Patti Page (he produced the latter's haunting "Hush, Hush, Sweet Charlotte") and had recently hit an amazing stride, producing Simon and Garfunkel's *Sounds of Silence* and *Parsley, Sage, Rosemary and Thyme*, as well as Bob Dylan's *Blonde on Blonde* and *John Wesley Harding*. Cash, feeling renewed after his recovery, decided to pursue a project that he had been after for years but that Columbia had flatly refused: to record a live album in a prison. In particular, he wanted to sing "Folsom Prison Blues" for the men in Folsom Prison, and he wanted America to hear how the men there responded to a sympathetic voice. When Cash told Bob Johnston that he had always found prisoners the most responsive and enthusiastic audience, Johnston said, "That's what we've got to do, first thing."

Cash had been playing prisons for more than a decade, since performing at Huntsville, Texas, in 1957. As he told the London *Daily Telegraph* near the end of his life, "I have a feeling for human nature in difficult situations. Don't know why, but I always have." Indeed, while other entertainers, including numerous country artists, had performed in prisons over the years, nobody had a better feel for playing in such desolate and perilous places, and certainly nobody had a keener sense of cultural timing, than Cash. This was the late 1960s, and in the face of rising fears about violent crime, civil rights protests and youthful unrest, various politicians, including 1968 presidential candidates George Wallace and Richard Nixon, were wield-

ing the easy slogan of "law and order" as a corrective measure — and as code for suppressing activism and branding the disenfranchised. It was in this context that the singer finally stepped onstage at Folsom on January 13th, 1968, and announced, "Hello, I'm Johnny Cash," then bolted into "Folsom Prison Blues," the prisoners roaring in recognition of the song's depictions of violence, remorse and defiance. The moment had tremendous resonance throughout American culture. Alongside "Folsom Prison Blues," even inflammatory songs like the Rolling Stones' "Street Fighting Man" and Jefferson Airplane's "Volunteers" seemed affected. Nobody else in popular music could match Cash for radical nerve or compassion.

*At Folsom Prison*, though, wasn't Cash's last word on the matter. On February 24th, 1969, he recorded a second prison album (and filmed a documentary special for British television), *At San Quentin*, which produced the biggest single of his career, a rendition of Shel Silverstein's novelty song "A Boy Named Sue." (In the time between the two prison appearances, Cash's longtime guitarist Luther Perkins suffered fatal burns. He was replaced by Bob Wootton by the time of the San Quentin

date.) Though the *Folsom Prison* album was more groundbreaking and generally featured better performances, the concert for San Quentin was regarded by all participants as the riskier affair. San Quentin was a notoriously bleak penitentiary. Cash had played there on previous occasions (including a 1958 performance that Merle Haggard, an inmate at the time, later

TWO VIEWS OF CASH'S *enchanting estate on Tennessee's Old Hickory Lake, where he lived for thirty-six years.*

described as "the first ray of sunlight in my life"), but for some reason, things were especially tense on that night in 1969. Cash prowled the stage restlessly. He taunted the guards. He ridiculed the prison system and its authorities. He commiserated with criminals and violent men and sang prayers for them, while guards paced on catwalks above the crowd, cradling loaded machine guns. In her liner notes for the reissued version of *At San Quentin*, June Carter Cash wrote, "Some kind of internal energy for those men, the prisoners, the guards, even the warden, gave way to anger, to love, to laughter. . . . A reaction like I'd never seen before. I was enraged inside, a feeling of fire, dangerously tense. And John sang quietly, 'San Quentin, you're livin' hell to me. . . .' 'Sing it, Cash! You know it, man, we're all in hell here!' 'So you give us the word, Cash, and we'll beat the hell out of them, just for the hell of it.' It took a while, maybe ten minutes, before he got to repeat the first and second line of his first-time-ever heard-of song, 'San Quentin. . . .' John held these men in suspense, they were mesmerized, hypnotized and spellbound, and so were we. . . . He held them by a thread, and we were saved by that thread." Cash later told journalist and author Bill Flanagan, "The guards were scared to death. All the convicts were standing up on the dining tables. They were out of control, really. During the second rendition of that song all I would have had to do was say 'Break!' and they were gone, man. . . . Those guards knew it, too. I was tempted."

Cash sometimes took heat for identifying himself with prisoners and prison reform. In a 1973 interview in *Country Music*, he said, "People say, 'well what about the victims, the people that suffer – you're always talking about the prisoners; what about the victims?' Well, the point I want to make is that's what I've always been concerned about – the victims. If we make better men out of the men in prison, then we've got less crime on the streets, and my family and yours is safer when they come out."

Years later, on Christmas Day, 1982, Cash found his ideals put to a hard test. He was spending the holiday with family members and friends at a home he owned in Jamaica. As the group was sitting down to dinner, three young men wearing nylon stockings over their heads – one brandishing a pistol, another a knife, the third a hatchet – burst in. They were rough with the women, put a gun to the head of Cash's son and demanded a million dollars. For the next few hours, Cash spoke to the men calmly, with measured respect. He convinced them there was no way he could get them that much money right then. He had a few thousand dollars in the house, though, and they could have it. They could also take all the valuables that were at hand. The men eventually assembled their loot and left, locking Cash and the others in the cellar. Before they left, the robbers gave the captives the Christmas dinner they had disrupted. That night, the Jamaican police captured the gunman and killed him on the spot. Weeks later the other robbers were caught, then killed when they allegedly tried to escape from prison. In his 1997 autobiography, Cash wrote that he had spent a good deal of time trying to come to terms with the knowledge that the "desperate junkie boys" who had menaced him and his family "were executed for their act – or murdered, or shot down like dogs. . . ." He didn't think he felt safer for their deaths. "My only certainties," he wrote, "are that I grieve for desperate young men and the societies that produce and suffer so many of them, and I felt that I knew those boys. We had a kinship, they and I: I knew how they thought, I knew how they needed. They were like me." And that comprehension, Cash believed, was what helped him and his family and friends avoid murder when it walked in their door that Christmas Day.

AT FOLSOM PRISON, 1968. *"If we make better men out of the men in prison, then we've got less crime on the streets, and my family and yours is safer when they come out."*

\* \* \* \* \* \*

N FEBRUARY 1969, Johnny Cash and Bob Dylan recorded several tracks together in Nashville, with Bob Johnston serving as producer. The two singers had been friends since the early part of the decade, when Cash wrote Dylan, telling him how much he liked his music. Since that time, Cash had served as a passionate advocate of Dylan's. In 1964, when *Sing Out!* – the magazine of the folk movement – published an open letter to Dylan, taking him to task for writing fewer protest songs, Cash wrote to the magazine, saying, "Shut up and let him sing!" A year later, at the Newport Folk Festival, when outraged folk purists tried to cut off the power as Dylan played a loud set of electric rock & roll, Cash was among those who blocked their efforts. "I don't

think anyone around today has so much to offer as him," he told one reporter at the time. And yet in mid-1969, when Dylan released his and Cash's lovely duet performance of "Girl From the North Country," on *Nashville Skyline*, the moment came as something of a shock to both the country and the rock & roll worlds. Observers on both sides wondered what the teaming signified. Why was Cash singing with rock's most revolutionary voice? Why would Dylan record in the country idiom, which at the time was seen as a music of conservative values and prejudice? There is a wonderful moment in Robert Elfstrom's 1969 documentary *Johnny Cash! The Man, His World, His Music,* during a duet on Dylan's "One Too Many Mornings" (a song about people who are alienated from one another), when Cash sings to Dylan, "You are right from your side, Bob/But I am right from mine," and Dylan grins back and says, "I know it." In that exchange, the two men acknowledged that there was room for more than one complex perspective among reasonable people in difficult times.

In 1970, Cash received a call from President Richard Nixon's office, inviting him to perform for an evening at the White House. Nixon's chief of staff, H.R. Haldeman (who would later resign and spend eighteen months in prison for his involvement in the Watergate scandal), had put together a list of requests. Among them were "Okie From Muskogee" (a Merle Haggard hit that took a dim view of youthful drug users and war protesters) and "Welfare Cadillac" (a Guy Drake song that derided the integrity of welfare recipients). Cash respected the office that Nixon held and also supported the U.S. troops in Vietnam (although after the U.S. assault on Cambodia, Cash talked about the war as a terrible waste of life). He could not, however, bring himself to sing the songs that Nixon requested. For one thing, they weren't his songs; for another, having grown up poor himself, he wasn't about to sing a song like "Welfare Cadillac," which he later described as a "lightning rod . . . for anti-black sentiment." Though Cash accepted Nixon's invitation, he insisted on picking his own material. "The show is already planned," he had his secretary tell Haldeman; he would perform for the president the same sort of show he performed for prisoners and everybody else. Later, introducing

Cash to the audience at the White House, even Nixon got the point. "One thing I've learned about Johnny Cash," he said, "is that you don't tell him what to sing."

To be sure, Johnny Cash was a complicated patriot, and those complications — like the contradictions of the nation itself — never ceased. Moreover, as Henry Pleasants wrote, Cash's "concern is people rather than ideas." Indeed, a varied thing. In the early 1970s, Cash performed for a progressive student body at Nashville's Vanderbilt University and, at the peak of the Vietnam War, debuted the song that came to be seen as his testimonial, "Man in Black": "I wear the black in mournin' for the lives that could have been/Each week we lose a hundred fine young men . . . /Well, there's things that never will be right, I know/And things need changin' everywhere you go . . . /But I'll try to carry off a little darkness on my back/Till things are brighter, I'm the Man in Black." Some fifteen years or so later, he stood before a much more conservative audience at Nassau Coliseum, in Uniondale, New York, and said, "I thank God for all the freedoms we've got in this country. I cherish them and I treasure them — even the right to burn the flag. I'm proud of those rights. But I tell you what, we've also got . . ." He paused, because the crowd had started booing loudly enough to drown him out, then he confidently hushed them. "Let me tell you something – shhh – we also got the right to bear arms, and if you burn my flag, I'll shoot you. But I'll shoot you with a lot of love, like a good American." It was a statement full of extraordinary twists and turns, genuine pride and dark-humored irony — and only Cash could get away with weaving such disparate stances and affectionate sarcasm together. When all was said and done, Johnny Cash looked at America the same way he looked at himself: with forthright regrets and unrelenting hope.

\* \* \* \* \*

N 1969, Johnny Cash was at the peak of his popularity. He began hosting a summer series for ABC TV, *The Johnny Cash Show*, which would feature such guests as Bob Dylan, Joni Mitchell, Ray Charles, Merle Haggard, Waylon Jennings, Louis Armstrong, James Taylor and Neil Young. The show — which was broadcast from Nashville's Ryman Auditorium, the residence of the Grand Ole Opry since 1943 — immediately enjoyed high ratings, and ABC renewed it as an ongoing series. By the year's end, according to Clive Davis (who was president of Columbia Records at the time), Cash had sold more than 6.5 million records and placed seven albums on the *Billboard* charts, more than any other recording artist in 1969. The next year, June Carter Cash gave birth to the couple's only child – and Cash's only son – John Carter Cash. But a short time later, en route to play for American troops in Vietnam, Cash lapsed back into drug abuse. It was a short but hard tumble ("I had been the most negative and evil man I could ever remember being," he wrote in *Man in Black*), and it wouldn't be his last one. He missed drugs, he admitted later in his life, and it sometimes took all his faith and will to carry that hunger without succumbing to it.

Then, in the early 1970s, everything shifted – and the shift lasted for a long time. Cash's music began to slip. His albums seemed tamer, more per- functory, and the big hits stopped coming. (After "Flesh and Blood" and "Sunday Morning Coming Down," both from 1970, Cash had

THE MAN IN BLACK, *onstage during an episode of his TV show in 1970*

only one major pop single in the ensuing decade, the 1976 song "One Piece at a Time.") He was also growing tired of the TV show; he felt that ABC executives were forcing too many artists on him who didn't fit his aims while denying him other guests. "I want them . . . to tell me why Pete Seeger can't be on my show," he said angrily to the show's director, according to a *New York Times Magazine* article. "Pete Seeger is a great American; he's sold the Appalachian Mountains in Asia. Why can't I have my friends on this show?" (Seeger had been severely criticized for his politics by the House Committee on Un-American Activities – which even declared him in contempt of Congress – and as a result of his ongoing opposition to the Vietnam War, network television refused to book him on any shows.) In 1971, ABC declined to renew Cash's contract.

As the 1970s progressed, Cash found that his brand of insurgent country was proving less provocative. The "outlaw" movement – made up of Willie Nelson, Waylon Jennings and Tompall Glaser, among others – was making its own hard-edged brand of country, mixing a storytelling sensibility with honky-tonk ethics, cowboy defiance and touches of rock & roll rhythm and tonality. The results riled Nashville's more conventionalist ethos but also influenced many other country and rock artists. Cash didn't begrudge the movement – after all, he had once helped displace

Nashville's weary standards himself, and Waylon Jennings was a longtime friend and one-time roommate. But he also knew that he was no longer at the center of the country music world, after more than a decade in which he had held sway as its most liberating and successful artist. A few years later, he found his music had been eclipsed again—this time by the successes of members of his own family. His step-daughter Carlene Carter, his oldest daughter, Rosanne Cash, and Rosanne's husband at the time, Rodney Crowell, all made vital and attention-grabbing progressive country music in the late 1970s and early 1980s. (Cash and his wife were fortunate enough—if that's the right term—to be present when Carlene Carter told a New York audience that she wanted to "put the cunt back into country.")

In the mid-1980s, Cash joined the two main leaders of the outlaw movement, Willie Nelson and Waylon Jennings, along with singer-songwriter Kris Kristofferson, for an all-star troupe called the Highwaymen. The group's recorded output was hit-or-miss (though *Highwayman* and *The Road Goes On Forever* featured some terrific moments), but their live shows were solid, and the four men's partnership met with good record and ticket sales. Even so, Columbia Records had little faith in Cash's on-going creativity, and various executives and producers pressured him to accommodate new styles that might appeal to contemporary country audiences, which were now viewed as liking their music with fewer rough edges. Cash was tired of trying to adjust to Columbia's demographics-driven concerns, and in 1986 he gave them a new song called "Chicken in Black," accompanied by a video in which Cash dressed as a chicken. His message was that if the label was being cowardly and wanted a chicken for an artist, then there was no point in making any bones about it. The song was also, Cash said, intentionally awful. Columbia dropped him. He wasn't selling, and the label wasn't interested in an album of just him and his guitar, which had been a pet project he'd pushed for years. He signed with Mercury, but it didn't want the guitar-and-voice album either. Cash did record two decent albums— *Johnny Cash Is Coming to Town* and *Boom Chicka Boom*—but the label still took little interest in them. Cash later said that he felt he had once again hit a low point. Life was turning hard. He fell back into addiction in the early 1980s—again involving pills and alcohol—until his family sent

him to the Betty Ford clinic. In 1988 he underwent double-bypass surgery and came close to dying. By the early 1990s, his albums sales had more or less dried up, and Columbia let all but a few of his albums disappear from print. Cash had given up wanting to deal with record companies, he said. He was resigned to playing places like Branson, Missouri—an entertainment center that is also sort of a hell's waiting room where aging pop and country performers play their glory-days hits for people looking for music that appeals to their sense of nostalgia. Cash had been a giant, but to the modern music business he was already a figure from history.

What Cash didn't anticipate—what nobody anticipated—was that he was about to embark on his most surprising period of artistic growth since the 1960s. More than that, he was about to pass through the most extraordinary winter phase of any major artist in the history of popular music.

\* \* \* \* \* \*

OHNNY CASH WAS perplexed when Rick Rubin first approached him in 1993. Rubin was a producer with his own label, American Recordings, and he was known for his pivotal support of hardcore hip-hop and rock & roll acts like the Beastie Boys, Danzig, Slayer, the Red Hot Chili Peppers and Public Enemy. Cash knew some of the music, or at least music akin to it. In the 1980s, when his son John developed a passion for Metallica, Cash attended some of the band's shows with his son and learned to enjoy some hard thrash music. Still, Cash couldn't fathom what interest Rubin might have in him or how they would work together. "[Rubin] was the ultimate hippie," Cash wrote in his second memoir, "bald on top but with hair down over his shoulders, a beard that looked like it had never been trimmed (it hadn't), and clothes that would have done a wino proud. . . . Besides, I was through auditioning for producers, and I wasn't at all interested in being remodeled into some kind of rock act." Rubin didn't see Cash as needing to fit a rock mold, or any other mold. In fact, Rubin understood something about the singer that no other music executive or producer seemed able to grasp at the time: namely, that Cash's influence ran deeper than any one tradition—he was an archetype of the outsider, the lonely figure with a dark side who changes everything for the better for everybody else — and that he still had the power to make important music. What Cash needed to do, Rubin knew, was figure out the songs he wanted to sing and then sing them — just him and his guitar. Nothing else should come between him, his spellbinding voice and the listener. "You'll come to my house . . . ," Rubin told Cash, "take a guitar and start singing. You'll sing every song you love, and somewhere in there we'll find a trigger song that will tell us we're headed in the right direction. I'm not very familiar with a lot of the music you love, but I want to hear it all." It sounded to Cash a lot like the philosophy that Sam Phillips brought to bear on their early sessions. It also sounded like an opportunity to make the record he had always wanted to make.

Maybe it was simply the way his worldview had taken on as much gravity and depth as his voice. Or maybe it was just a demonstration of how life adds up — how it gives and takes, then takes and gives. In any event, Cash's first work with Rubin, 1994's *American Recordings*, had an effect like no other album Cash had ever made. It was a collection of songs (by writers like Tom Waits, Glenn Danzig, Kris Kristofferson, Leonard Cohen, Loudon Wainwright III and Cash himself) about betrayal, murder, love, death, fear of oneself, faith, more death, rootlessness, deliverance, death again, and life and vengeance after death. The trigger song — in this case literally — that Rubin had been looking for turned out to be "Delia's Gone," Cash's vicious and heartbroken rewrite of a folk-blues song that went at least as far back as Southern blues singer Blind Willie McTell in the 1920s. Cash had taken three earlier, lyrically identical passes at the song in the 1960s, yet the *American Recordings* version was so unadorned and plaintive that its matter-of-factly brutal first-person narrative about a man killing the woman he loves shocked some listeners, especially in the moments that Cash sang, "I found her in her parlor and I tied her to her chair . . ./First time I shot her, I shot her in the side/ Hard to watch her suffer, but with a second shot she died." It even shocked MTV, which refused to air the song's video, in which Cash heaps dirt on Delia (played by model Kate Moss). Cash told author Nick Tosches that the more traditional, historical versions of the song were "not quite as bloody and criminal-minded. . . . I just decided I'd make this man who kills Delia a little bit meaner than he already was. Tie her to the chair before he shoots her. Have a little

more fun with her." In the end, Delia has the last word. In jail, the cell door locked, the night coming down, the killer lies awake, listening to Delia pacing around his bed. "Delia's Gone" may have been unnerving, but it was an effective reminder that folk music — the wellspring for blues, country and rock & roll — was at heart a weird and scary music, full of dark American secrets.

*American Recordings* sold more copies than any other Cash work in years, ranked high in numerous critics' year-end lists and appealed to a whole new younger audience that was unafraid of bleak musings and that also saw Cash as a rare exemplar of integrity and authenticity. In the years that followed, this newfound audience — which included fans of alternative music of all sorts — proved as loyal to Cash and his recordings as his rural and working-class audiences had in decades before. In the meantime, *American Recordings* enjoyed little country radio airplay and received no Country Music Association Award nominations. In fact, the only time Cash received any CMA recognition (before a belated, sentimental outpouring at the organization's 2003 awards show) was in 1969. Though many in the country world had continually appreciated Cash, plenty of others had always been uncomfortable with his renegade spirit and his freethinking social concern, and radio programmers in particular were decidedly not enamored of the spare style and the disquieting outlook of his new music. So in the 1990s, they treated him as an artist who no longer made music. In 1998, when his *Unchained* album won a Grammy for Best Country Album, Cash took out another of his full-page *Billboard* ads. It read, "American Recordings and Johnny Cash would like to acknowledge the Nashville music establishment and country radio for your support." The words appeared alongside a famous 1969 photo of Cash at San Quentin, flipping a "fuck you" middle finger directly into the camera's lens, with a fierce scowl on his face.

Cash, though, couldn't appear at the Grammys to accept his award for *Unchained*, the second of his albums with Rubin. The singer had been walking down Madison Avenue in New York in October 1997 when he found himself involuntarily walking backward. He saw a doctor and was told to go home to Nashville immediately and get into a hospital. He contracted blood poisoning and double pneumonia and almost died, and he stayed near death for ten days. He recovered, only to learn he'd been diagnosed

with Shy-Drager syndrome, a neurological disorder that is a worse variation of Parkinson's disease. He improved enough to return to performing. But then, one night onstage in Flint, Michigan, his guitar pick slipped from his fingers. He leaned over to retrieve it but almost fell. The audience was unsure of what was going on. A few people laughed—and then Cash told them he had Parkinson's. "It ain't funny," he said. "It's all right. I refuse to give it some ground in my life." The Shy-Drager and Parkinson's diagnoses would turn out to be incorrect—Cash in fact had autonomic neuropathy, a disorder of the nervous system. But by the time he received the 1998 Grammy, he could no longer make public appearances and had quit touring after forty-two years on the road. In addition, any more recordings seemed unlikely. Some doctors didn't think he could live another year. But Cash and Rubin recorded new sessions whenever possible. The work was fitful, brought to a halt several times by bouts of pneumonia, the onset of diabetes and a ten-day coma that nobody thought Cash would come out of.

Against all reasonable odds, Cash's last two albums, *American III: Solitary Man* (2000) and *American IV: The Man Comes Around* (2002), are damn near the best music he ever made—and certainly his bravest and most chilling. Cash's voice shows more age and vulnerability, though it rarely sounds frail. Indeed, his singing on parts of *Solitary Man* is astonishing. In his versions of Will Oldham's "I See a Darkness" and Nick Cave's "The Mercy Seat," he sings like a man in his worst hour of desperate prayer, discovering a voice he never knew he had before as a show of strength, though his heart and mind are plunging into despair and chaos. But in all of Cash's American recordings, there is nothing as revealing as his version of Nine Inch Nails' "Hurt," from *The Man Comes Around*. "Hurt" is the story of a man who suffers more for all the ways he makes others suffer. In fact, it is a song about an addict who looks unblinkingly at the worst truth he has ever encountered—the abyss of his own heart: "What have I become, my sweetest friend/Everyone I know goes away in the end/You could have it all, my empire of dirt/I will let you down, I will make you hurt." Cash knew this territory well. He had mapped it, ransacked it and even tried to crawl off and die inside its caves, and now he was describing unsparingly what he had learned of himself in his darkest recesses.

In the end, Cash's American Recordings series stands alongside his best music for Sun in the 1950s and for Columbia in the 1960s. It is resourceful music that details how a man grows and deteriorates at the same time, as he bears witness to all he finds painful and promising in the world that he is living and dying in. It is all the more remarkable given that, as he made this music, everything was slipping away from Cash—everything except his integrity and the love of the woman who kept faith in him even when he could not stand his own heart, who did everything she knew to keep him alive. "She's . . . certainly made me forget the pain for a long time, many times," he once said. "When it gets dark, and everybody's gone home and the lights are turned out, it's just me and her."

Then it was just him.

\* \* \* \* \*

OR YEARS, June Carter Cash was seen as the necessary balance in her husband's life—the woman who fought for his intrinsic worth, who stood by him, onstage and in their personal life, offsetting his grave image with down-to-earth verve. She also brought a blistering sexuality to his music. Her famous song about their love affair, "Ring of Fire," was infused with an uncommon mix of biblical language and metaphors of lust. And when she and Johnny performed their live duet of "Jackson," they turned the song's story of romantic ennui into an enactment of mutually overpowering erotic need.

June never objected to her image as her husband's steadfast helpmate. "I chose to be Mrs. Johnny Cash," she said in 1999. "I decided I'd allow him to be Moses, and I'd be Moses' brother, Aaron, picking his arms up and padding along behind him." Yet June Carter Cash was a formidable figure in American music in her own right—not only as an heir of the Carter Family tradition but as an artist who might

have extended it. "The Kneeling Drunkard's Plea," which she co-wrote, served as a key model for the sort of keenly observed songs of compassion that her husband himself would aim to write throughout his career. As Johnny once noted, "She started at the age of nine and has spent more years on the stage than even Bill Monroe had when he died.

Sadly, I think her contribution to country music will probably go underrecognized simply because she's my wife; it certainly has been up to now. That's regrettable – my only regret, in fact, about marrying her."

On *Press On*, the 1999 album that was June's first solo release in decades, there is a fascinating track called "I Used to Be Somebody," in which she talks about her friendships with James Dean, Tennessee Williams and Hank Williams and her rumored affair with Elvis Presley. As the song unfolds, she seems to come to an understanding of all that she left behind to become the wife of a man as overwhelming as Johnny. "Well, I used to be somebody, Lord," she sings, "I used to have a friend/I'd like to be somebody again/I used to be somebody, dear Lord, where have I been?/I ain't ever gonna see Elvis again." No doubt June was resolved and fulfilled in the choices she made, though being married to Johnny Cash could not have always been an easy thing. In 2000, she wrote, "I'm still searching deeper into the soul of this man for the light that shines somewhere within him" – but maybe there had to be a bit of darkness in June herself in order to attract and withstand Johnny. Theirs was no doubt a real marriage: passionate, volatile, full of secret hurts and private fervor, and an unending prayer that they would stay in the presence of each other until they died.

On May 7th, 2003, June Carter Cash underwent a heart valve replacement at Nashville's Baptist Hospital. Severe complications set in after surgery, and on May 15th she died, at age seventy-three. So many of us had grown accustomed to keeping a watchful eye on Johnny's health that it never seemed likely that June would be the first to leave. The closest anybody came to suggesting as much was June herself, in a recording session for her 2003 album, *Wildwood Flower*. In her version of the Carter Family's "Will You Miss Me When I'm Gone?" she sings, "When death shall close these eyelids/And this heart shall cease to beat/And they lay me down to rest/In some flowery-bound retreat/Will you miss me – miss me when I'm gone?" It was a lovely and blue rumination about one of the most heartbreaking prospects the dying can face, and there could be no doubt about the answer the song's question raised.

At June's funeral, Johnny had to be helped from his wheelchair to view his wife's face one last time. At a family gathering, he said, "I don't know hardly what to say tonight about being up here without her. The pain is so severe, there is no way of describing it." A few days after June's burial, Johnny called Rick Rubin and told him that he wanted to get back to recording songs as soon as possible. "I don't want to do anything of this world," Cash said. "I want to make music and do the best work that I can. That's what she would want me to do, and that's what I want to do." In the next few months, Cash recorded more than fifty new tracks, including some original material and versions of black gospel songs like Blind Willie Johnson's "John the Revelator."

Despite his determination and hard work, Cash reportedly could not recover from the loss of his wife. Guitarist and singer Marty Stuart – Cash's close friend and former son-in-law (he had once been married to Cash's daughter Cindy) – told *Time* that in his last months Cash would sometimes break down into deep sobs, saying, "Man, I miss her so bad." Stuart also told *USA Today* that in Cash's last months, a pair of vultures had started sitting outside the window of the singer's Hendersonville office, staring at Cash as Cash stared back. In late August, Cash planned to attend the MTV Video Music Awards in New York, where "Hurt" had been nominated for six awards, including Video of the Year, but his health made the trip impossible. When the Best Male Video prize went to Justin Timberlake for "Cry Me a River," the young pop star told the audience, "This is a travesty. . . . My grandfather raised me on Johnny Cash and I think he deserves this more than any of us tonight." Several days later, Cash suffered some respiratory problems and was admitted to Baptist Hospital. On September 12th, 2003, after a nearly fifty-year career, John R. Cash breathed his last breath, at age seventy-one, due to respiratory failure brought on by diabetes. Three of his surviving siblings and three of his five children were at his bedside. One of the last recordings he made was a duet with his daughter Rosanne. In the rawest voice to be heard in any of his recordings, he sang:

I plan to crawl outside these walls
Close my eyes and see
And fall into the heart and arms
Of those who wait for me
I cannot move a mountain now
I can no longer run
I cannot be who I was then

In a way, I never was. . . .
They will fly me like an angel
To a place where I can rest
When this begins, I'll let you in
September when it comes.

I NEVER MET JOHNNY CASH, but I did speak with him once, on the worst day of my life.

I grew up in a family that agreed on very little — especially when it came to whether to respect or hate one another — but one thing we managed to share was a love for Johnny Cash and his music. My mother had grown up with country music, my older brothers came of age to early rock & roll, my father sequestered himself with opera, and I had my own passions for Bob Dylan and Miles Davis — yet something in Cash's voice and stories spoke to us across our differences. I'm sure it had to do with his image as country music's angry man and the fact that he stood up for underdogs.

I had a brother named Gary — ten years older than me. He had been in and out of jails since he was fourteen, and spent all but a few months of his adult life in prison for armed robbery. I didn't always feel close to Gary. Sometimes he scared me. Sometimes I hated him. And worse, sometimes I loved him. But when Cash put out *At Folsom Prison* in 1968, it couldn't help but make me think of my brother and how he loved Cash even more than the rest of us. It also made me think about what his daily life behind bars must really be like. I tried sending him a copy of the record for Christmas that year, but the authorities wouldn't allow him to have it.

In 1976, following his parole from prison, on consecutive summer nights in Utah, my brother murdered two innocent men during armed robberies, in a mix of drugs, alcohol and cold, pain-filled rage. He was arrested, tried, convicted and sentenced to death, and he demanded that the state carry out the sentence it had handed him. Nobody had been executed in America in almost ten years. That meant that if Gary's demand was granted, America would be back in the business of putting select criminals to death. Johnny Cash was opposed to the death penalty. He didn't make a big point of it, but he also didn't pretend otherwise. When he heard that my brother was a fan of his music, he issued a dignified plea to Gary, asking him to reconsider his decision. He also sent him a copy of his autobiography, *Man in Black*, along with a letter in which he restated his plea. "They've already killed too damn many of us," he wrote, describing his view of the prison system and executions. Gary appreciated Cash's attention, but he was determined to die. On the last night of his life, my brother received a phone call from his favorite singer. Later that night, in my last conversation with Gary, I asked him what Cash had said. Gary said, "When I picked up the phone I said, 'Is this the real Johnny Cash?' And he said, 'Yes, it is.' And I said, 'Well, this is the real Gary Gilmore.'"

The next day, in the hours after Gary's execution, I sat around my house trying to understand how I would be able to live with the horrible things my brother had done and the horrible way he had died. I had already written some articles for Rolling Stone at that time, and my editor, Ben Fong-Torres, called me that afternoon and said, "Johnny Cash would be willing to talk to you." I called the number Ben gave me; it was a recording studio in Nashville. In moments Cash was on the phone, talking to me in that familiar low voice. I told him, "I just wanted to thank you, on behalf of my mother and myself, for the help and comfort you offered my brother. I know it helped him at the end. I just wanted to . . ." And then I couldn't talk anymore. I was just feeling too awful, too awkward, too afraid of falling apart. "That's all right, son," said the low voice at the other end. "I know you and your mother tried. We all tried. I'm sorry for what has happened. I know how much this must hurt right now, but I hope in time you can find some peace. Our prayers are with you."

I don't know that I ever found the peace that Cash wished me that day, but I know that in those moments he took to speak with me, I found something that made as much difference as anything might on that impossible day: I heard a voice — from a man who had always represented courage and dignity in my family's mind — offer a stranger understanding and kindness, without any judgments. That was more grace than I expected or perhaps deserved from somebody who wasn't a friend in those hours, and I have always been grateful for it.

Cash didn't have to talk to me that day. He didn't have to talk to any of us in America about those forces or impulses that hurt and bewildered us. But he chose to anyway, and he did it not because doing so made him a better person but rather because he wasn't always a better person himself, and he knew he had to understand the meaning of that truth at least as much as the meanings of faith or piety. For something good to come from all the times he had fallen, all the times he had risked his health and sanity and spirit, the times he had let down those who loved or trusted or needed him, he had to comprehend his own history and heart. In 1994 he said, "I think anybody would be making a mistake if they didn't recognize that they have a dark side or a side that isn't really good." By recognizing his own dark side, Cash also came to acknowledge how others who were lost or angry, or who were feeling just plain fucked-up, might arrive at the worst choices in their lives. He did this in part to find ways to control his own darkness, but he also did it to find ways to speak to or about other people, with a voice that might make a difference.

Johnny Cash doesn't have to try to manage darkness anymore — he is in it now, whatever its nature might be, whether it is of God or of nothing. He's out there with a lot of other good and bad men, with the ghosts of poets and fugitives and all those somewhere in between. He had a way of speaking to them all.

We won't get another like him, and we know it. We are likely too far down the line from the histories and conditions and experiences that shaped him and others like him. That old America has truly melted away into fable. But we do get to hold on to Cash's voice — that revealingly imperfect voice that ran so deep, in so many ways. It will continue to sing to us, to help us along from time to time, as we make our way through the dark places in our own hearts, and through those uneasy American nights still to come.

CASH, IN OCTOBER 2002. *He recorded more than fifty new songs in the final year of his life.*

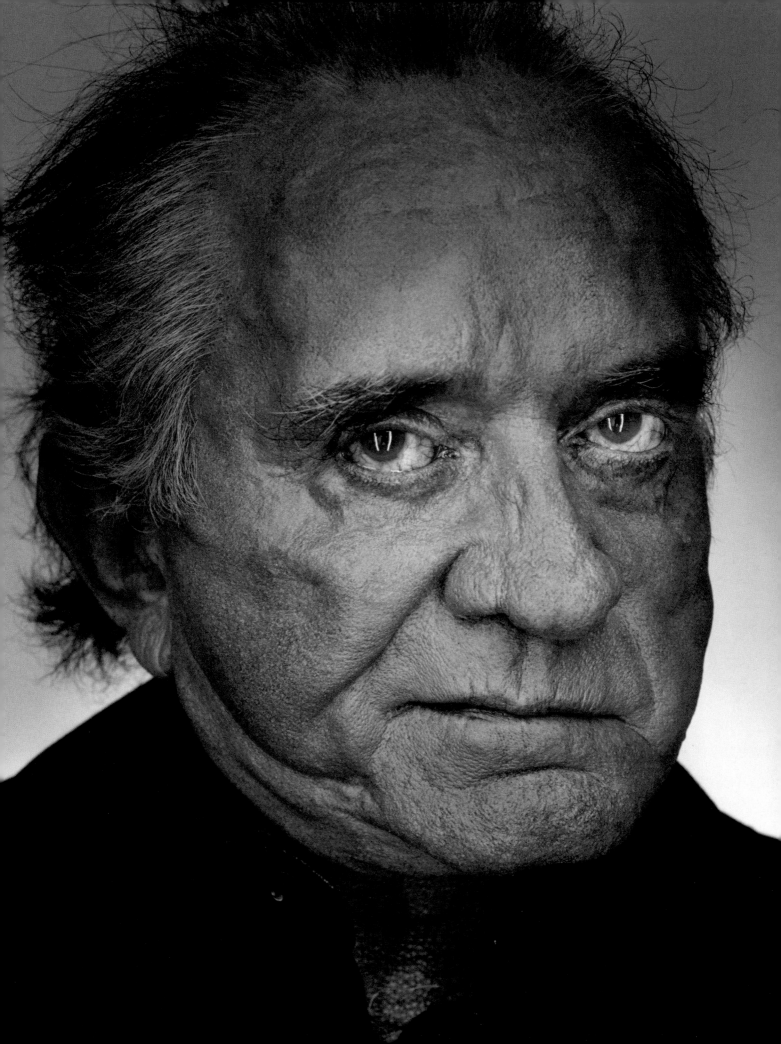

# GROWING UP POOR

### By
## JOHNNY CASH

*From "Cash: The Autobiography"*

THE FIRST SONG I remember singing was "I Am Bound for the Promised Land." I was in the back of a flatbed truck on the road to Dyess, Arkansas, from the first house I remember living in: the place next to the tracks out in the woods near Kingsland, Arkansas, where my family had ended up after a succession of moves dictated by the rigors of the Depression. That was a real bare-bones kind of place, three rooms in a row, the classic shotgun shack. It shook like the dickens every time a train went by. It wasn't as bad as the house I'd been born in, though. I don't remember living in that one, but I saw it once when I went to visit my grandfather. It was a last resort. It didn't have windows; in winter my mother hung blankets or whatever she could find. With what little we had, my parents did a lot.

The new house toward which the flatbed truck was taking us was something else, a brand-new deal of the New Deal. Late in 1934, Daddy had heard about a new program run by the Federal Emergency Relief Administration in which farmers like him who had been ruined by the Depression were to be resettled on land the government had bought. As he explained it in later years, "We heard that we could buy twenty acres of land with no money down, and a house and barn, and they would give us a mule and a cow and furnish groceries through the first year until we had a crop and could pay it back, and we didn't have to pay

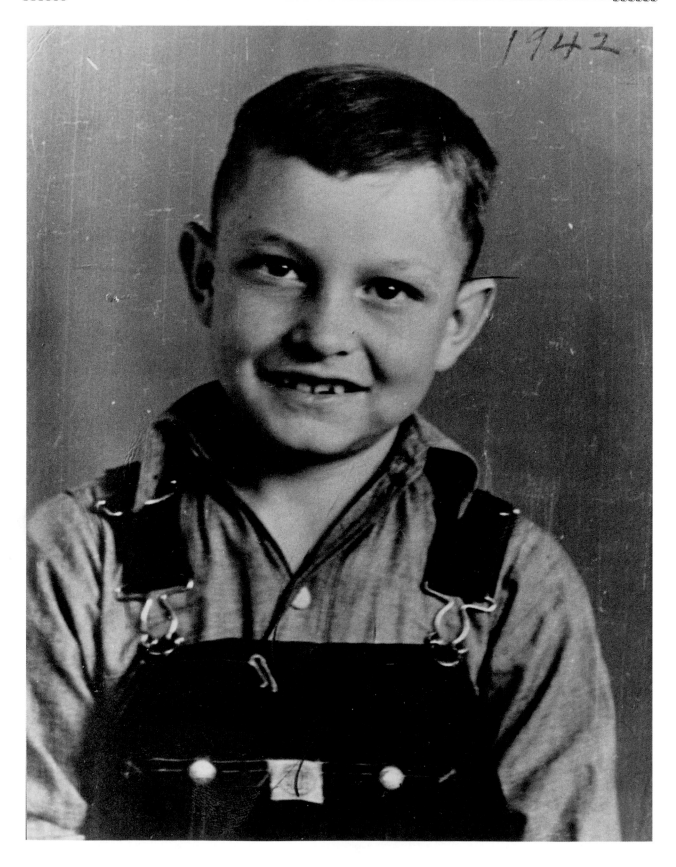

until the crops came in." That's exactly what the deal was, and more: In forty-six different places in the agricultural United States, these "colonies" were being created on a cooperative basis. In the settlement toward which we were headed, we and all the other families would have a stake in the general store, the cannery, the cotton gin and other facilities; we were all responsible for them and we all shared in their

profits, if any. Our new community was named after the administrator of the FERA program for Arkansas, W.R. Dyess. All in all, it covered about 16,000 acres of delta bottomland in Mississippi County. It was laid out like the spokes of a wagon wheel. Our place was Number 266, out on Road Three, about two and a half miles from the center.

I remember coming to that house so clearly. It took us two days to travel the 250 miles from Kingsland, first on gravel roads and then on dirt roads turned to mud by a hard, bitterly cold rain. We had to stop overnight by the roadside in the truck the government had sent for us, and we kids slept in the back with just a tarpaulin between us and the rain, listening to Moma cry and sing.

*By the time he was in fourth grade in 1942, Cash was already working the cotton fields with the rest of his family.*

Sometimes Moma would cry and sometimes she'd sing, and sometimes it was hard to tell which was which. As my sister Louise put it later, that was one of the nights when you couldn't tell. It all sounded the same.

When we finally got to Dyess, the truck couldn't get up the dirt road to our house, so Daddy had to carry me on his back the last hundred yards through the thick black Arkansas mud – gumbo, we called it. And that's where I was when I saw the Promised Land: a brand-new house with two big bedrooms, a living room, a dining room, a kitchen, a front porch and a back porch, an outside toilet, a barn, a chicken house *and* a smokehouse. To me, luxuries untold. There was no running water, of course, and no electricity; none of us even dreamed of miracles like that.

The next day, Daddy put on a pair of hip waders and went out to take stock of our land. It was jungle – I mean real jungle. Cottonwood and elm and ash and hickory as well as scrub oak and cypress, the trees and vines and bushes tangled up so thick in places that you couldn't get through, some of it underwater, some of it pure gumbo – but Daddy could see its potential. "We've got some good land," he said simply when he came back, with an air of hope and thanks we could all feel. That was a significant remark.

The land was awfully hard to clear, but Daddy and my oldest brother, Roy, then almost fourteen, went at it from dawn till nighttime six days a week, starting on the highest ground and working their way downward foot by foot, cutting with saws and axes and kaiser blades – long-handled machetes – and then dynamiting and burning out the stumps. By planting season the first year they had three acres ready. Two went for cotton, a cash crop Daddy would use to make his first payment to the government, and the other went for animal feed and food for our table: corn, beans, sweet potatoes, tomatoes and strawberries.

The crops came in well that first year, and the Cashes were on their way. The following spring I was five and ready for the cotton fields.

You often hear Southern musicians of my generation, black and white, bluesmen, hillbilly singers, and rockabillies alike, talking about picking cotton (and doing whatever it took to get out of the cotton fields), but I've sometimes wondered if the people listening to us, who are usually younger and/or more urban than we are, have any real grasp of the life we're talking about. I doubt if most people these days even know what cotton is, beyond being a comfortable kind of fabric. Maybe they'd like to know. Maybe *you* would, if only as musicological background. Huge swatches of the blues and country music do after all come from the cotton fields in a very real way: Many a seminal

Dyess High School
PUPIL'S INDIVIDUAL SUBJECT REPORT CARD

NAME *J. R. Cash*

DATE *1948-49*   GRADE *11*

### GRADES FIRST SEMESTER

| SUBJECT | 1 | 2 | 3 | Av. | Exam. | Sem. |
|---|---|---|---|---|---|---|
| English 4 | B | D+ | B- | C+ | D+ | C- |
| CONDUCT | A | A | A | A | | A |
| EFFORT | B | C | C- | C+ | | C+ |
| TIMES TARDY | 0 | 0 | 0 | | | 0 |
| DAYS ABSENT | 2 | 3 | 3 | | | 8 |
| TEACHER | John C. Gamble | | | | | |

### GRADES SECOND SEMESTER

| SUBJECT | | 2 | 3 | Av. | Exam. | Sem. |
|---|---|---|---|---|---|---|
| English 4 | D- | C- | D+ | D | D | D |
| CONDUCT | A | A | A | A | | A |
| EFFORT | B- | C | D | C | | C |
| TIMES TARDY | 0 | 0 | 0 | | | 0 |
| DAYS ABSENT | 3 | 0 | 2 | | | 5 |
| TEACHER | John C. Gamble | | | | | |

### SIGNATURE OF PARENT

| | |
|---|---|
| 1st Report | Ray Cash |
| 2nd Report | Ray Cash |
| 3rd Report | Ray Cash |
| 4th Report | Ray Cash |
| 5th Report | |
| 6th Report | |

ging a cotton sack. We didn't carry those nice baskets like you see in the movies; we used heavy canvas sacks with tar-covered bottoms, six feet long if you were one of the younger children, nine feet long for big kids and grown-ups. Going at it really hard for ten hours or so, I could pick about three hundred pounds; most days it was more like two hundred.

It's true, there really wasn't much to recommend the work. It exhausted you, it hurt your back a lot, and it cut your hands. That's what I hated the most. The bolls were sharp, and unless you were really concentrating when you reached out for them, they got you. After a week or two your fingers were covered with little red wounds, some of them pretty painful. My sisters couldn't stand that. They got used to it, of course — everybody did — but you'd often hear them crying, particularly when they were very young. Practically every girl I knew in Dyess had those pock-marked fingers. Daddy's hands were as bad as anyone else's, but he acted as if he never even noticed.

*LEFT: CASH's eleventh-grade report card — always on time, but a poor English student. BELOW: J.R., 17, photographed at the state fair in Memphis.*

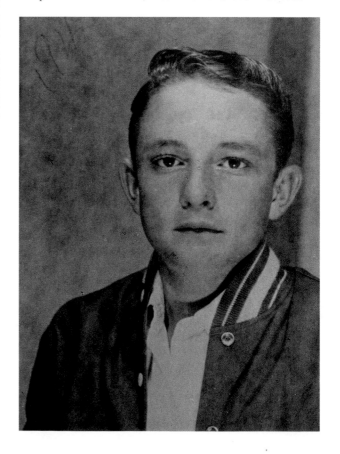

song was actually created there, and even more were spread from person to person.

Here, then, is how it went with cotton and us: We planted our seeds in April, and if we worked hard enough and our labors bore fruit and the Big Muddy didn't rise and the army worms didn't come through and no other natural disasters were visited upon us, the first blooms opened on plants that were four feet high in October. We began picking soon after that, though we couldn't pick efficiently until a killing frost had stripped the leaves off the plants and made the bolls easier to see. Picking lasted on through December, when the winter rains started coming and the cotton started turning dark, descending in quality and losing its value as it did so.

I started out in the fields as a water boy, which is just how it sounds: You tote drinking water to the grown-ups and older children. By the time I was eight, though, I too was drag-

*WITH HIS FATHER, Ray, and mother, Carrie, in 1970. Carrie, whose father had been a church musician, taught her children to sing in the fields.*

Come August and its doldrum heat, we had what we called laying-by time and for a two- or three-week period we'd work only three days a week in the cotton fields. That, though, was the time for digging potatoes, cutting hay and hauling it to the barn, and all that stuff. So there was never really any end to it; the work just went on and on. We did get ahead with the cotton, and that was the thing: Whatever else happened, you stayed ahead with the cotton.

There were, of course, forces against which we were powerless. The Mississippi was foremost in that regard — my song "Five Feet High and Rising" came from my own experience, not some storybook — but other acts of nature could and did wipe out a whole year's worth of your work and income. For instance, we did once get in the way of army worms. They moved in massive congregations, millions of them, and had an effect on the land in their path just like Sherman's boys had on Georgia. They went from field to field, eating — eating *fast* — and then moving on, and there was nothing you could do about them. You could stomp them all you wanted, all day and all night too if it made you happy, but that wouldn't get you anywhere even close to making a difference. Army worms were the bane of every cotton farmer in Arkansas. Now, wouldn't you know, they barely cross anyone's mind; you just spray for them and forget about it.

That's not to say that modern farmers don't have plenty to worry about. They sure do, and they always will. But I bet they also have some of the same great pleasures that lit up my young life. When the cotton began to open in October, for instance, it was just beautiful. First there'd be lovely white blooms, and then, in about three days, they'd turn to pink, whole fields of them. What a picture that was.

That wasn't all, either. Under those pink blooms there'd be tiny, tender little bolls, and they were such a sweet treat. I used to pull them off and eat them while they were still tender like that, before they began turning fibrous, and I loved them. My mother kept telling me, "Don't eat that cotton. It'll give you a bellyache." But I don't remember any bellyache. I remember that taste. How sweet it was!

# THE
# SUN
## SESSIONS

*By*

## DAVID FRICKE

OHNNY CASH WAS
an official Sun Records artist for three
years, three months and twenty-five days:
from March 22nd, 1955, to July 17th, 1958,
according to the tape-reel notations, musicians union contracts and in-house paper-
work kept in haphazard fashion by the
label's founder and chief producer, Sam
Phillips. In that whirlwind time, Cash wrote
and recorded more than half a dozen of his

most famous songs, racked up eleven Top Five country smashes and four Top Twenty pop singles, and transfigured Southern rural working-class song with the moralistic dignity of his storytelling and the conquering-warrior boom of his baritone voice.

But Cash did not make history every day in Sun's storefront studio, at 706 Union Avenue in Memphis, Tennessee. First takes of early glory such as "Hey Porter" and "Folsom Prison Blues" reveal a nervous, uncertain Cash, with only a nascent awareness of the rare, theatrical force of his singing. And guitarist Luther Perkins – half of Cash's skeletal backing group, the Tennessee Two, with bassist Marshall Grant – plays his simple licks with an apprehensive tension that often spills out in fluffed notes and tempo stumbles, even on master takes.

Phillips – smarting from the November 1955 loss of his greatest discovery, Elvis Presley, to RCA – made his share of mistakes in recording and selling Cash as a pop idol; the 1957 embarrassment "Ballad of a Teenage Queen" is the most excruciating chart buster to bear either Cash's name or Sun's iconic rooster-and-sunrise logo. And when Cash defected to the established promotional muscle and greater creative latitude of a major label the following year, he raced through his lingering obligations with unseemly haste, cutting nearly a third of his entire Sun catalog – mostly ill-fitting covers, since he was hoarding originals

PREVIOUS PAGE: SAM *Phillips presents Cash with his gold record for "I Walk the Line."* ABOVE: *The 78 of "Ballad of a Teenage Queen/Big River," cut November 1957.*

for his Columbia Records debut – in the last three months of his deal.

Yet on the dates examined here, Cash's intuitive gifts and Phillips' generous wisdom trumped circumstance and commerce. Cash's Sun recordings let us hear, up close, the explosive growth of one of America's greatest singer-songwriters and the legendary Sun studio aesthetic in all its raw, revolutionary splendor. "We went with what we had," Cash said of his Sun days in a 1992 ROLLING STONE interview, "and never gave it a second thought that we needed anything else."

* * * * * *

## MARCH 22ND, 1955

OHNNY CASH'S FIRST golden era began when he bushwhacked Sam Phillips at Sun's front door. "I was sitting on the stoop just as he came to work, and I stood up and said, 'I'm John Cash, and I want you to hear me play,' " Cash recalled in Peter Guralnick's book *Country Music.* "He said, 'Well, come on in.' I sang two or three hours for him. Everything I knew."

This was not unusual at Sun. As a producer, Phillips was a studio auteur in the same pioneering league as Phil Spector and George Martin: a man of great technical invention and creative empathy. As a fisher of talent,

Phillips was closer to the folklorists John and Alan Lomax: a keen listener and an exhaustive documentarian of common men and women, whom he recorded, often at great length, in his search for the uncommon. Located at the crossroads of plantation and hillbilly cultures, run by a businessman who preferred integrity to polish, Sun was an urban magnet for country dreamers. Cash was no exception. He also passed the Sun studio every day on his way to broadcasting school.

We may never know exactly how much time passed between that doorstep ambush and Cash's first real Sun session. According to one account, Phillips told Cash to return the next day with Perkins and Grant. Phillips himself claimed that he auditioned Cash a couple of times before seriously rolling tape. And in their sessionography for the 1990 Bear Family collection of Cash's Sun recordings, *The Man in Black 1954-1958*, Sun scholars Colin Escott and Martin Hawkins dated a surviving tape of four solo Cash demos back to late 1954, suggesting that Phillips devoted unusual care and patience to developing Cash – and his songs – for release.

The formal start of Cash's life at Sun is astonishing for both its magic and its comic disappointment. On March 22nd, he and the Tennessee Two bolt through one take of "Hey Porter" at lunatic speed, as if Cash were running to catch the train instead of impatient to jump off, while Perkins hits an embarrassing patch of indecision in one of his two jittery guitar breaks. And Phillips rejected that day's stab at "Folsom Prison Blues." The band rushes through the song practically at bluegrass tempo, and Cash delivers the signature line – "I shot a man in Reno/Just to watch him die" – at a throwaway cadence.

But a version of Cash's "Wide Open Road" that went unissued for many years is noteworthy for a lesson learned. A local pedal steel guitarist, thought to be A.W. "Red" Kernodle, overwhelms the terse interplay between Cash's voice, Perkins' guitar and Grant's bull fiddle with busy whining licks. After that, the pedal steel player was gone, either of his own accord or having been dismissed by Phillips. Phillips later described his approach to recording Cash this way: "I didn't want anything to distract from the command that Johnny had with the sound of his voice."

Phillips attained that stark perfection on March 22nd with the keeper take of "Hey Porter." Cash wrote the lyrics while he was in the Air Force, stationed in Germany, and you can hear a desperate homesickness reverberating inside his baritone. The rest of the track is just the huff and rattle of a train under full steam: Cash's acoustic guitar buzzing between Grant's churning bass and the metallic canter of Perkins' guitar.

Cash had his Sun sound in place – but, by Phillips' standards, only one releasable performance. Several weeks later, Cash returned to Sun with the A side of his debut single. He, Perkins and Grant reportedly spent thirty-five takes nailing "Cry, Cry, Cry" – a figure that belies the song's aggressive simplicity. Cash sings his merciless put-downs with a triumphant vengeance, and Perkins heightens the attitude with crisp, contrapuntal guitar. Perkins' elementary walking lead, doubled at the end by Grant's bass, is a paragon of country-blues pith. A shy, limited musician, Luther was no relation by blood or ability to Sun's other guitar-playing Perkins, Carl. But every note Luther played, good or bad, was an honest one – a reflection of the roots and integrity of the men making this music.

* * * * * *

### JULY 30TH, 1955

CASH DID NOT WRITE the whole of "Folsom Prison Blues," another souvenir of his time in Germany. He naively borrowed half of the lyrics and melody from a 1953 song by Gordon Jenkins, "Crescent City Blues." Jenkins did not get around to suing for payment or credit until 1968, when Cash recut "Folsom Prison Blues" in concert at the actual facility. But on this date, in the summer of 1955, Cash truly owns the searing heartbreak in the song.

The differences between the March 22nd misfire and this definitive execution are many. The pace is slower. Perkins is in firm control of his ping-pong riff. Cash's acoustic guitar jangles like leg irons, and he sings with a heavy, thoughtful syncopation – the rhythm of a man condemned to shuffle from his cell to the exercise yard every day for the rest of his life. Cash has also discovered the emotionally manipulative power in his voice. He drops down to bottom-floor bass as he sings the last lines: "And I'd let that lonesome whistle/Blow my blues away." The contrast between the image of a screaming locomotive and those vocal notes, rumbling up from a well empty of all hope, is breathtaking.

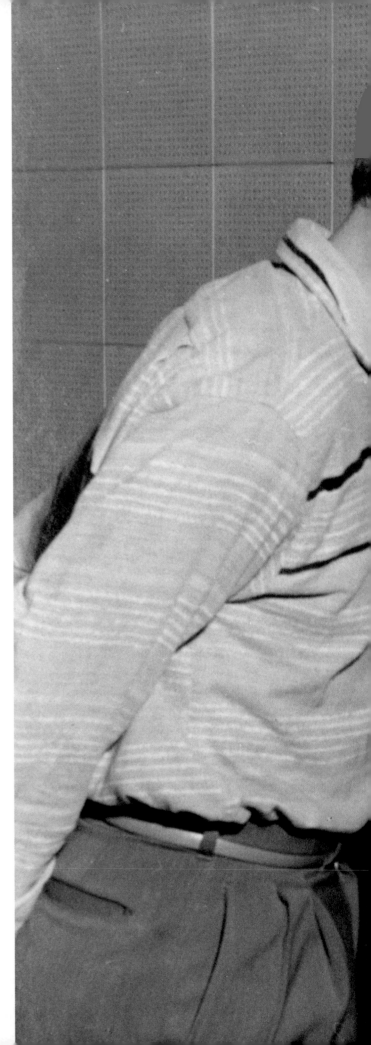

"Mean Eyed Cat" is another you-dirty-rat romp – "Folsom Prison Blues" crossed with "Cry, Cry, Cry." In "So Doggone Lonesome," which became the flip side of "Folsom Prison Blues" on Sun 232, Phillips lightens up on the echo, as if he's still trying to figure out the right balance of earthquake and atmosphere, notes and shadows, in this strange gothic barn-dance music. And you can't help but laugh at, and be touched by, Cash's droll tribute to his struggling guitarist in "Luther Played the Boogie." In the verses, Cash describes the kind of show he and the Tennessee Two would deliver nightly on the bandstand: railroad songs, blues, ballads, "jump 'n' jive." "But the thing that knocked them off their feet," Cash sings, "was when Luther played the boogie-woogie [*repeated eight times!*] in the strangest kind of way." At that point, Luther plays nothing stranger than a stair step melody, gingerly, in unadorned single notes.

"I saw something in the plaintiveness of Luther's picking," Phillips said in Colin Escott and Martin Hawkins' 1991 Sun history, *Good Rockin' Tonight.* "I said, 'John, it's worth it, you know.' " Phillips was right. "Musicians scoffed," Escott and Hawkins wrote, "but Cash and the Tennessee Two possessed the quality that had been lacking in country music since Hank Williams died: originality."

\* \* \* \* \* \*

### APRIL 2ND, 1956

HE CLIMAX OF Cash's first year at Sun, this session produced both sides of his best single for the label: Sun 241, "I Walk the Line"/"Get Rhythm." He wrote the former in fifteen minutes while on tour with Carl Perkins. One night in Gladewater, Texas, Cash was messing around on a guitar with an unusual chord progression, yet another product of his time in Germany. An admiring Perkins asked him what he was playing, then encouraged him to turn it into a song. Later, when the chatter turned to the subject of married musicians and bedroom mischief on the road, Cash remarked, "Not me, buddy. I walk the line." Perkins, another straight arrow, replied, "There's your song title."

"I Walk the Line" is more mantra than song: a chantlike pledge of fidelity held together by little more than Cash's

THE MILLION DOLLAR *Quartet, from left: Jerry Lee Lewis, Carl Perkins, Elvis Presley and Johnny Cash – Sun's biggest stars – got together once, on December 4th, 1956.*

hypnotic strum and Luther Perkins' ticktock lick. The key modulations and the sustained *ommm* of Cash's voice at the start of each verse are at once peculiar and irresistible – Gregorian church song and Buddhist prayer wrapped in farmer's denim and rolled down a dirt road.

There is also a startling swing in Cash's step: On earlier records, he had inserted a folded piece of wax paper between the strings of his Martin guitar, creating a subtle percussive undertow, like the swirl of brushsticks on a snare drum. (Phillips took credit for the idea.) Here, that trick is front and center in the mix. With the chords totally muted on his guitar and Perkins picking as if in a trance, Cash carries everything in "I Walk the Line" – gratitude, pride, lust, responsibility – with elegant vocal gravity. When he first heard the results on the radio, though, he was seized by second-guessing; he felt he could have done better, that the rhythm was too fast. He called Phillips, asking him to withdraw that version and replace it with a slower take. Thankfully, Phillips vetoed the request.

In "Get Rhythm," Cash sounds just as serious – about having fun. For Cash's first Sun release, Phillips had taken the liberty of professionally christening the singer "Johnny," thinking it would be good bait in the burgeoning teenage market. (Cash's parents had simply named him J.R.; the Air Force, apparently phobic about initials, made him John.) But Cash was a stone-country anomaly among the ducktail rockers and Presley wanna-bes crowding Sun's roster in the late Fifties. His attempts to write straight-up rockabilly tunes were few and generally disastrous. (A notable exception: "Rock & Roll Ruby," cut with vigor in early 1956 by another Phillips discovery, Warren Smith.)

But "Get Rhythm" is high-stepping blues with country-guitar cluck, a jubilant prescription for salvation by beat: "Get a rock & roll feeling in your bones/Put taps on your toes and get gone." The star of the song is a shoeshine boy, "bending low at the people's feet/On a windy corner on a dirty street." The lad's defiant cheer, despite his social station and the weather, is the lyric engine, with the slapping sound of his brush and cloth echoed in Perkins' riffing and the wax-paper sizzle of Cash's rhythm guitar.

Cash allegedly wrote "Get Rhythm" for Elvis Presley, but he wisely kept it for himself. The gritty existentialism of "I Walk the Line" put Cash in the pop Top Twenty for the first time. With the added pow of "Get Rhythm," Sun 241 became Cash's first gold record.

O N THE DAY he recorded his least distinguished Sun hit, Cash was already on his way to another label. In California, late in the summer of 1957, he and touring partner Carl Perkins had met English-born producer and Columbia A&R man Don Law, who asked if the pair would consider coming to the company after their respective Sun deals ended. Clandestine negotiations ensued, even as Phillips was preparing to issue Sun's first-ever twelve-inch LP: *Johnny Cash With His Hot and Blue Guitar*, a peculiar roundup of early singles and recent covers, including Leadbelly's "Rock Island Line" and Vernon Dalhart's railroad weeper "Wreck of the Old 97."

In fact, Cash was writing fewer hits. His sales and chart numbers had fallen from their 1955 and '56 highs. And Phillips had started delegating production duties to Jack Clement, a new Sun staff member. Clement was an aspiring composer himself. He also believed Cash's records suffered from a lack of sugar.

On July 1st, 1957, Cash and the Tennessee Two cut a version of "Home of the Blues," a song Cash titled after a popular Beale Street store where, in pre-stardom days, he used to buy Robert Johnson and Sister Rosetta Tharpe records. A few weeks after the session, Clement took the liberty of loading the trio's no-frills track with drums, piano and a male vocal chorus, in blatant imitation of the uptown gloss of Elvis Presley's RCA recordings. Distortion created by Clement's overdubbing scarred the final master. Still, "Home of the Blues" squeaked onto *Billboard*'s pop chart. It was all the precedent Clement needed.

By November 12th, Cash – who had just recovered from throat surgery – was actually recording a Clement song, a cheesy tale about a high school beauty who leaves town to become a Hollywood star but ultimately returns to settle down with a nice neighborhood boy. In the hands of a watered-down Elvis like Pat Boone, "Ballad of a Teenage Queen" would have been merely irritating. Forced on Cash, someone who had vividly written and sung of murder, hard time and true commitment, it was an insult.

Cash threw himself into "Ballad of a Teenage Queen" with as much decorum as he could muster. The initial take – just Grant, Clement on acoustic guitar and Cash's voice, embedded in echo – is a surprising pleasure, if you ignore the story and the nagging references to "The boy next door/Who worked at the candy store." But ten days later, Clement added the fatal sweetening: a glee-club-style chorus ("Dream on, dream on, teenage queen") fronted by the wordless, faux-operatic birdsong of soprano Cyd Mosteller.

To Clement's credit, he made a hit record with big-city gloss under the relatively primitive studio conditions at Sun. And the payoff was immediate. Cash was soon touring Canada in the dead cold of December and hosting "Teenage Queen" contests at each stop. Sun sold 100,000 copies of the single across Canada in a little more than two weeks. (In Saskatoon, Cash arrived to crown the local "Teenage Queen" winner, only to find out that she had died; instead, the honor went to the runner-up — a young Joni Mitchell.) When the single broke wide open in the U.S. at the start of 1958, the sales and airplay propelled the B side — Cash's "Big River," also cut on November 12th — onto *Billboard*'s pop chart as well.

Inspired by a magazine headline — JOHNNY CASH HAS THE BIG RIVER BLUES IN HIS VOICE — "Big River" is a swaggering act of pride, Cash's portrait of himself as a force of nature: "Now, I taught the weeping willow how to cry/And I showed the clouds how to cover up a clear blue sky." And Clement underscores the rushing-water metaphor by stuffing the space between Perkins' guitar and Grant's bass with surging acoustic rhythm guitar. A year earlier, "Big River" would have been a top-flight A side on its own. But twinned with Clement's cotton candy — and compared with the high-speed hellfire of Sun's newest star, Jerry Lee Lewis — the song and performance felt righteous yet ancient, a throwback to a nobler, purer Sun. "Big River" was the last great record Cash made for Sun — even though he would keep cutting tracks there, running out the clock, for eight more months.

\* \* \* \* \* \*

N JULY 17TH, 1958, Cash paid his last working visit to 706 Union Avenue, sleepwalking through four numbers — two Clement songs, Charlie Rich's "I Just Thought You'd Like to Know" and a relic: Elvis Presley's last Sun single, "I Forgot to Remember to Forget" — with Perkins, Grant, Rich on piano, Sun session drummer J.M. Van Eaton and rockabilly flash Billy Riley on guitar. Exactly seven days later, Cash

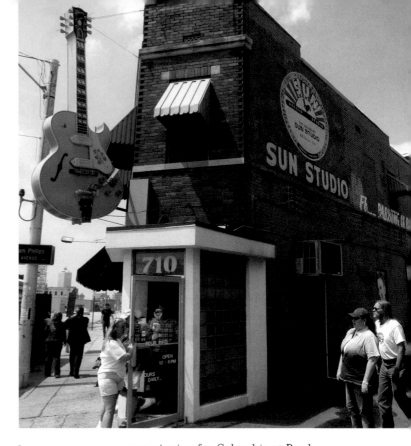

SUN STUDIOS IS NOW A museum and one of Memphis' most popular attractions.

was singing for Columbia at Bradley's Film and Recording Studio in Nashville. His first golden era was over; the second, during which he would transform and rule country music for more than twenty years, had begun.

But Cash never forgot what he achieved at Sun. Indeed, nearly four decades after he first confronted Sam Phillips on the sidewalk, Cash started making records with the same attention to emotional purity and elementary detail with a much younger man, producer Rick Rubin. "He told me that Sam and I were the only people to ask him to play all of his songs, who wanted to hear everything he had," Rubin said of Cash in an interview shortly after Cash's death. "He said that he'd never really had that in Nashville. Everyone there seemed to have an agenda for him, an idea of what they wanted him to do.

"A large part of the producer's job," Rubin went on, "is to create a safe environment for the artist to do his best work and be himself, to be vulnerable and expose his true self, without commercial or personal constrictions."

Rubin was describing his own approach to recording Cash during the final ten years of the singer's life. It is also a perfect description of how Phillips and Cash — together, at their best — challenged each other, made hit records and changed popular music history, during those three years, three months and twenty-five days.

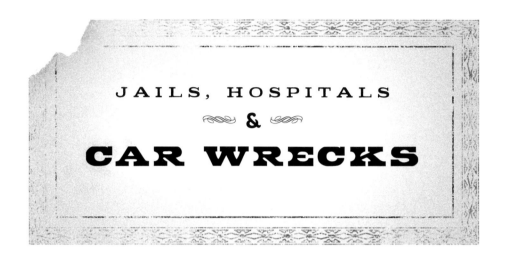

## JAILS, HOSPITALS

### &

# CAR WRECKS

By

## JOHNNY CASH

*From "Cash: The Autobiography"*

# I took my first amphetamine,

a little white Benzedrine tablet scored with a cross, in 1957, when I was on tour with Faron Young and Ferlin Husky, and I loved it. It increased my energy, it sharpened my wit, it banished my shyness, it improved my timing, it turned me on like electricity flowing into a light bulb.

Every pill I took was an attempt to regain the wonderful, natural feeling of euphoria I experienced the first time, and therefore not a single one of them, not even one among the many thousands that slowly tore me away from my family and my God and myself, ever worked. It was never as great as the first time, no matter how hard I tried to make it so.

That doesn't mean it didn't feel good, though, and for a while the pills did their job just fine without too many obvious consequences. Doctors were prescribing them freely in those days for just the reasons I said I wanted them—to drive long distances, to work late hours—and though in truth I was taking them for the feeling they gave me, I started

by taking them only when I had to travel and/or do shows. People in the music business, the people I worked with, got the idea right from the start that I was high all the time, but that was only because I was high all the time when I was around *them*.

It felt great while I was high, but even in those first days the mornings after weren't so hot. I'd wake up and the guilt would slap me in the face. I'd remember something truly stupid I said to somebody, something insane and destructive I did. I'd realize that I'd forgotten to call home and say goodnight to my girls. Of course, sometimes that would feel so bad that I'd have to take another pill or two just to feel OK again. Gradually the binges grew longer, the crashes worse, the periods of sobriety shorter.

It wasn't long until the crashes got really bad. As soon as I woke up, I started feeling little things in my skin, briars or wood splinters, itching so badly that I had to keep trying to pluck them out; I'd turn on the light to see them better, and they weren't there. That kept happening and got worse — they started to be alive, actually twitching and squirming in my flesh—and that was unbearable. Then I had to take more pills. I talked about it to other people who used amphetamines, but nobody else had the problem for the simple reason that nobody else was taking as many pills as I was.

In the early 1960s the American Medical Association began waking up to the perils of prescribing unlimited amphetamines for anyone who wanted them, and getting drugs started getting to be work, especially for a traveling man. It got harder than simply calling the hotel doctor and having him send over sixty pills. If I was going on a ten-day tour, I had to plan accordingly, and that could be complicated. How many prescriptions did I have? Four? Four times sixty divided by ten, make that twelve just in case, is . . . hmmmm, maybe not enough. Maybe I needed another local source. Maybe I should call another doctor before I left. Maybe I should drive to that druggist forty miles away and get a hundred or two under the counter. Maybe I should call a friend, or friends, and ask them to go get a new prescription. Ultimately, I might have to rely on whatever I could find on the road.

Amphetamines are hard to handle, and once you're into them to any extent you find out very quickly that you have a pressing need for other chemicals. I soon had to drink alcohol, usually wine or beer, to take the edge off my high if it got too sharp or knock myself out after being up for days, and after a while I got into barbiturates, too.

I wasn't high *all* the time. Sometimes nothing I did would keep me in pills, and I'd be stuck somewhere out on the road, having to go clean. I feared that more than I feared my own death, but when it happened, I'd begin to feel pretty good after two or three days without drugs. Then, though, I'd get home, usually on a Monday, and I'd find the stress of my marriage so hard that I'd drive to that druggist, get two or three hundred pills, head out into the desert in my camper and stay out there, high, for as long as I could. Sometimes it was days.

I just went on and on. I was taking amphetamines by the handful, literally, and barbiturates by the handful too, not to sleep but just to stop the shaking from the amphetamines. I was canceling shows and recording dates, and when I did manage to show up, I couldn't sing because my throat was too dried out from the pills. My weight was down to 155 pounds on a six-foot, one-and-a-half-inch frame. I was in and out of jails, hospitals, car wrecks. I was a walking vision of death, and that's exactly how I felt. I was scraping the filthy bottom of the barrel of life.

By early October 1967, I'd had enough. I hadn't slept or eaten in days, and there was nothing left of me. I never wanted to see another dawn. I had wasted my life. I had drifted so far away from God and every stabilizing force in my life that I felt there was no hope for me.

I knew what to do. I'd go into Nickajack Cave, on the Tennessee River just north of Chattanooga, and let God take me from this earth and put me wherever He puts people like me.

You can't go into Nickajack Cave anymore. The Army Corps of Engineers put a dam in, which closed off the entrance we used. It was an amazing place, an opening 150 feet wide and fifty feet high into a system of caves, some of them bigger than two or three football stadiums, that ran under the mountains all the way down into Alabama. I'd been there before with friends, Bob Johnston once, Hank Williams Jr. another time, exploring and looking for Civil War and Indian artifacts. Andrew Jackson and his army had slaughtered the Nickajack Indians there, men, women and children, and soldiers from both sides of the War Between the States had taken shelter in the caves at various times during the conflict. The remains of the dead among them were joined by the bones of the many spelunkers and amateur adventurers who'd lost their lives in the caves over the years, usually by losing their way, and it was my hope and intention to

join that company. If I crawled in far enough, I thought, I'd never be able to find my way back out, and nobody would be able to locate me until I was dead, if indeed they ever could. The dam would be going in soon.

I parked my jeep and started crawling, and I crawled and crawled and crawled until, after two or three hours, the batteries in my flashlight wore out and I lay down to die in total darkness. The absolute lack of light was appropriate, for at that moment I was as far from God as I have ever been. My separation from Him, the deepest and most ravaging of the various kinds of loneliness I'd felt over the years, seemed finally complete.

It wasn't. I thought I'd left Him, but He hadn't left me. I felt something very powerful start to happen to me, a sensation of utter peace, clarity and sobriety. I didn't believe it at first. I couldn't understand it. How, after being awake for so long and driving my body so hard and taking so many pills — dozens of them, scores, even hundreds — could I possibly feel *all right*? There in Nickajack Cave I became conscious of a very clear, simple idea: I was not in charge of my destiny. I was not in charge of my own death. I was going to die at God's time, not mine.

I started crawling in whatever direction suggested itself, feeling ahead with my hands to guard against plunging over some precipice, just moving slowly and calmly, crablike. I have no idea how long it took, but at a certain point I felt a breath of wind on my back and knew that wherever the breeze was blowing from, that was the way out. I followed it until I began to see light, and finally I saw the opening of the cave.

When I walked out, June was there with a basket of food and drink, and my mother. I was confused. I thought she was in California. I was right; she had been. "I knew there was something wrong," she said. "I had to come and find you."

During the following days I moved through withdrawal to recovery. I retreated to the house I'd just bought on Old Hickory Lake. June and her mother and father formed a circle of faith around me, caring for me and insulating me from the outside world, particularly the people, some of them close friends, who'd been doing drugs with me.

At first it was very hard for me. It was the same nightmare every night, and it affected my stomach — I suppose because the stomach was where the pills had landed, exploded and done their work. I'd be lying in bed on my back or curled up

on my side. Then all of a sudden a glass ball would begin to expand in my stomach. My eyes were closed, but I could see it. It would grow to the size of a baseball, a volleyball, then a basketball. And about the time I felt that ball was twice the size of a basketball, it lifted me up off the bed to the ceiling. When it would go through the roof, the glass ball would explode and tiny, infinitesimal slivers of glass would go out into my bloodstream from my stomach. I could feel the pieces of glass being pumped through my heart into the veins of my arms, my legs, my feet, my neck and my brain, and some of them would come out the pores of my skin. Then I'd float

back down through the ceiling onto my bed and wake up. I'd turn over on my side for a while, unable to sleep. Then I'd lie on my back, doze off, get almost asleep – and the same nightmare would come again.

Eventually – slowly, with relapses and setbacks – I regained my strength and sanity and I rebuilt my connection to God. By November 11th, 1967, I was able to face an audience again, performing straight for the first time in more than a decade at the high school in Hendersonville, my new hometown. I was terrified before I went on, but surprised, almost shocked, to discover that the stage without drugs was not the frightening place I'd imagined it to be. I was relaxed that night. I joked with the audience between numbers. I amazed myself.

JOHNNY CASH WAS on a dazzling creative and commercial roll in the early Seventies when he followed Elvis Presley as the headliner in the Las Vegas Hilton's main show-room. His two live prison albums (*At Folsom Prison* and *At San Quentin*) had rejuvenated his career, and he hosted an ABC TV show whose guest list included some of the great country and rock artists of the day, including Bob Dylan, Joni Mitchell, Waylon Jennings and Merle Haggard.

Still, many in Las Vegas considered the Hilton booking a risky move because Cash's independent, blue-collar stance was so far from the town's mainstream — and he showed no signs of compromise. Cash didn't use a comedian to open the show

## NOTHING CAN TAKE THE PLACE of the HUMAN HEART

### By ROBERT HILBURN

(something even Presley did), and he didn't employ the house orchestra (something everybody did in Vegas). He brought his own musicians (the Tennessee Three, Carl "Blue Suede Shoes" Perkins, the Statler Brothers and, of course, June Carter). He not only packed what was then the town's biggest showroom nightly, he also drew standing ovations after each performance.

For this interview, we first talked after one of his midnight shows in the thirtieth-floor penthouse the Las Vegas Hilton pro-vided for entertainers, and again over breakfast. He was pleased that ROLLING STONE would be interested in a country artist: "I've often read those interviews and wondered if they'd be interested in someone like me."

RS 129 • MARCH 1, 1973

*Music seems to have been an important part of your life from the beginning. What was the first time you remember listening to music?*

The first time I remember was my mother playing the guitar. Before I started school. I was four or five years old, but I remember singing with her. Carter Family songs, a lot of them. I don't remember any of them in particular, but I know they were gospel songs, church songs.

*You had to work on the farm when you were a kid. Was that an important part of your character building?*

Hard work? I don't know. Chopping cotton and picking cotton is drudgery. I don't know how much good it ever did me. I don't know how much good drudgery does anybody.

*I get the feeling, though, that you have empathy with people who work hard, that you want to reassure them in your music that their life has meaning.*

Yeah. I got a lot of respect for a man that's not afraid to work. I don't think a man can be happy unless he's working. And I work hard on my music. I put in a lot of thought. I lose a lot of sleep, a lot of nights, because I'm laying awake thinking about my songs and about what's right and what's wrong with my music. I worry about whether that last record was worth releasing, whether I could have done it better. Sometimes I feel that the last record was exactly like the one I released fourteen years ago. I wonder if I'm just spinning my wheels sometimes. I wonder if I'm progressing, if I'm growing musically, artistically. I guess I've quoted Bob Dylan a million times, his line "He who is not busy being born is busy dying." I've always believed that. And I believe it is certainly true in my case.

Even though I'm forty years old and I'm getting a little gray hair on my head, I'm still growing. You're being born a little bit every day. And I love performing. It's my first love. I love performing even more than writing. And something you love, you try to do well.

*Going back to your early childhood, what was the next step – musically?*

I started writing songs myself when I was about twelve. I started writing some poems and then made some music up to go along with them. They were love songs, sad songs. I think the death of my brother Jack, when I was twelve, had a lot to do with it. My poems were awfully sad at the time. My brother and I were very, very close.

*Did you sing the songs to your family? What was the reaction?*

Oh, well, you know how families are. My dad would pat me on the head and say that was pretty good, but you'd better think about something that will buy you something to eat someday. My mother was 100 percent for my music. When I was sixteen she wanted me to take piano and voice lessons. She even took in washing to get the money. I think I had the voice lesson. The teacher told me not to take any more because it might affect my delivery.

*What was the first time you sang in public?*

I guess it was at high school commencement. I sang Joyce Kilmer's "Trees." I had a high voice, a tenor when I was a teenager. I had just piano accompaniment. I was pretty scared. I didn't do anything else until after I got out of the Air Force.

*Did you have a feeling at that time, when you went into the Air Force, that you were ever going to really get into music?*

Yeah, I always knew. I really did. I always knew. I remember writing my father when I was in the Air Force, telling him that I'd be recording within a year after I was discharged. I wrote "Folsom Prison Blues" while I was in the Air Force in Germany. I wrote it one night after seeing a movie called *Inside the Walls of Folsom Prison.* I also wrote "Belshazzar" and "Hey Porter" in the Air Force.

*When you got to Memphis, how did you get into the music business?*

I found out about Sun Records in Memphis. They were getting pretty hot with Elvis about that time, so I called about an audition. I remember how scared I was the first time I walked into Sun. It was Sam Phillips and his secretary, Miss McGinnis. They didn't even remember I had an appointment to record. I got the first of seven "come back laters." I told Phillips that I wrote gospel songs. I thought "Belshazzar" was the best song I had to show him. He said, "Well, the market is not too good for gospel songs. Come back sometime when you feel like you've got something else."

But we eventually got together, and I believe we recorded "Hey Porter" the same day. The first session was really something. Luther Perkins had a little secondhand Sears amplifier with a six-inch speaker. Marshall Grant had a bass that was held together with masking tape. I had a $4.80 guitar that I had brought back from Germany. Phillips had to be a genius to get anything out of that conglomeration.

*How did the Johnny Cash sound come about?*

That *boom-chicka-boom* sound? Luther took the metal plate off the Fender guitar and muted the strings because he said he played it so ragged that he was ashamed of it and he was trying to cover up the sound.

*How did you feel when you had the first record in your hand? It must have been a big day for you.*

It was the most fantastic feeling I ever had in my life. I remember signing the recording contract the day the record was released. I had both the contract and "Hey Porter" in my hand when I left Sun that day. And I had fif-teen cents in my pocket. I remember coming out of the studio and there was a bum on the street. I gave him the fifteen cents. That's true. Then, I took the record to the radio station, holding it like it was an old master painting. And the disc jockey dropped it and it broke. By accident. It was the next day till I could get another one. That was really heartbreaking. But the record went on to get a lot of airplay, especially in the South. Presley's first manager, Bob Neal, called me and wanted me to do some concerts with Elvis. The first place I played was Overton Park, in Memphis. I did "Hey Porter" and "Cry, Cry, Cry," and the reaction was good, very good.

*"I Walk the Line" was the big record for you. Did you have a special feeling about it when you finished it?*

I thought it was a very good song, but I wasn't sure about the record. I was in Florida when I first heard it on the radio, and I called Phillips and begged him not to send any more copies out. I thought it was so bad. I thought it was a horrible record. And he said, let's give it a chance and see. But I didn't want to. I wanted it stopped right then. I got upset with him over it. I thought it sounded so bad. Still sounds bad.

*What was it like returning home to Arkansas after you had become famous?*

Well, I was still the country boy to those people. I mean, I wasn't anything special to them. A lot of places I'd go in those days made you feel like the big radio star that I had wanted to be, and it felt good. I really ate it up. But at home all the old people would come up and say, "Boy, I remember when you used to bring me buttermilk every other Thursday," or something.

WITH ELVIS PRESLEY, *1957. Early in his career, Cash was the opener at several Elvis shows.*

*Was there a point that you ever lost touch with those people? During the bad years? Was there a point where you really didn't think of them as friends anymore?*

Yes, right. I felt like I didn't belong, and for about seven years I didn't go back. I didn't go back around those people. I didn't want any of them to see me.

*That was the bad time for you, the pills and all.*

Yeah, not too long after I moved to California. I still don't know why I ever moved to California. I liked it there, had worked out there quite a bit and thought I'd love living there. But I didn't really belong out there. I never really felt at home there. I tried to, but I just didn't. I got into the habits of amphetamines. I took them for seven years. I just liked the feel of them.

*Was it the lift?*

Yes, it lifts you, and under certain conditions it intensifies all your senses — makes you think you're the greatest writer in the world. You just write songs all night long and just really groove on what you're doing, digging yourself, and keep on taking the pills. Then, when you sober up later, you realize it wasn't so good. When I run across some of the stuff I wrote, it always makes me sick . . . wild, impossible, ridiculous ramblings you wouldn't believe.

You took more pills to cover up the guilt feelings. And I got to playing one against the other, the uppers against the downers, and it got to be a vicious, vicious circle. And they got to

pulling me down. On top of that, I thought I was made of steel and nothing could hurt me. I wrecked every car, every truck, every jeep I ever drove during that seven years. I counted the broken bones in my body once. I think I have seventeen. It's the grace of God that one of those bones wasn't my neck.

Over a period of time, though, you get to realizing that amphetamines are slowly burning you up, and burning you up is the truth — because they are hot after a while. Then you get paranoid, you think everybody is out to do you in. You don't trust anybody — even the ones who love you the most. It's like a bad dream now.

*Weren't there times you missed the shows regularly during those years?*

I got to where I had chronic laryngitis because I kept myself so dried out. And my voice would go and stay gone. I'd feel sorry for myself, and I'd go off and hide somewhere — up into the mountains or the woods. And the more I'd go, the worse I'd get.

*Was there a point that you think you hit bottom? Like the time in Georgia when you woke up in jail?*

Yeah, that was in '67. That's when things started turning. But that was just one of many awakenings I had. You know, that one has been written up in a lot of books and magazines, but that was just one of dozens or hundreds of times that I started reawakening and realizing that there was something good that was going to happen to me, that I had to pull myself out, that life was going to take a turn for the better.

I'd had seven years of roughing it, and I felt I had seven years of good times and good life coming. I really felt in 1967 that there were seven big years ahead.

*How did you start pulling out of those bad times?*

Well, it really started about the time June and I got married. The growth of love in my life and the spiritual strengthening came at about the same time. Religion's got a lot to do with it. Religion, love, it's all one and the same as far as I'm concerned, because that's what religion means to me: It's love. About the time I married June, we started growing in spiritual strength together. And it shows up onstage.

You can't fool the audience. You can't fool yourself. If you're not yourself onstage, it shows. I'm really happy now. But that's not the same as being content. I still want to grow more as a performer, as an artist, as a person. So, I'm still working hard at it. I never go on that stage when I'm not scared. There's always that fear that somebody's going to throw eggs at you or something.

*How would you get yourself up physically and emotionally for a recording session during those troubled years?*

I missed a lot of sessions. I'd come into the studio with a fog over my head, not really caring what condition I was in. Just go in on sheer guts and give it a try. It showed up on a lot of my recordings.

*But you were still able to come up with a quality product.*

I managed somehow. Something like the *Bitter Tears* album was so important that I managed to get enough sleep to do that one. [Songwriter and *Broadside* magazine contributing editor] Peter LaFarge and [folk singer] Ed McCurdy and I spent about three days together, talking and deciding that I needed some rest before I did the album. And I got the rest. I think *Bitter Tears* was one of my best works.

*I've read that you once listed LaFarge and Dylan as two of the biggest influences on your outlook and style as a songwriter. Is that true?*

Well, there was a time I guess they influenced me quite a bit. Of course, Dylan is going to influence anybody that is close to him, as a writer, some way or another. He's a powerful talent. But the influences in my life come and go and there's always something fresh coming along. There's always a change taking place. I don't know what the influences might be right now.

There's a lot to be said for music and friends. We were talking about the bad times earlier – the pills and things. And why I took them. I know why I took them now. It was to try and get a high like I naturally do now. I knew it was there and I thought I could get it on pills. But you can get it without pills, because the greatest times I remember were with my friends at my house – Dylan, Joni Mitchell, Kris Kristofferson, Mickey Newbury were all at the house one night, all those great songs.

*What was it about Dylan that attracted you?*

I thought he was one of the best country singers I had ever heard. I really did. I dug the way he did the things with such a country flavor and the country sounds. "Talkin' World War III Blues" and all those things on the *Freewheelin' Bob Dylan* album. I didn't think you could get much more country than that. Of course, his lyrics knocked me out, and we started writing each other. We wrote each other letters for about a year before we ever met.

I was playing here in Las Vegas the first time I heard one of his albums. I played it backstage, in the dressing room, and I wrote him a letter from here telling him how much I liked his songs, and he answered it and in so many words told me the same thing. He had remembered me from the days of "I Walk the Line" when he was living in Hibbing, Minnesota. I invited him to come see me in California, but when he came to California later he couldn't find my house.

I got another letter that was written in Carmel, and by the time I answered it, he'd already gone back to New York. When I was in New York not long after that, John Hammond told me that Bob was in town. So he came up and we met at Columbia Records. We spent a few hours together, talking about songs, swappin' songs, and he invited me up to his house in Woodstock. After the Newport Folk Festival, he invited me to his house again.

*Some people say that Dylan is aloof or withdrawn, that he is hard to talk to. Did you find him that way?*

We never did really talk all that much. There's a mutual understanding between us. I never did try to dig into his personal life and he didn't try to dig into mine. If he's aloof and hard to get to, I can understand why. I don't blame him. So many people have taken advantage of him, tried to do him in when they did get to him, that I wouldn't blame him for being aloof and hard to get to. Everybody tells him what he should write, how to think, what to sing. But that's really his business.

*Let's talk about your own songs. Do you have any special memories about them?*

Sure, most of my songs bring back memories. Things like how I happened to write them, where I was when they were released and so forth.

"Train of Love" – I remember writing that in 1955 when I was on the *Louisiana Hayride* show in Shreveport. Sam Phillips happened to be there. And I called him into the dressing room and asked him what he thought about the song. He really liked it. We recorded it on the next session.

"Home of the Blues" – that was the name of a record shop in Memphis and I always liked the name. Thought it was a great name for a song, so Glen Douglas and I wrote a song about it.

I wrote "Give My Love to Rose" about ten blocks from San Quentin Prison. I was playing a club there one night in '56, the

first time I came to California. And an ol' boy came backstage,
an ex-con, to talk to me about Shreveport. He was from there.
And I'm not sure his wife was named Rose, but his wife was in
Shreveport and he said something about "giving my love to
my wife if you get back to Shreveport before I do." He had just
gotten out of prison. I wrote the song that night.

"Big River" – I wrote it as a real slow bluesy thing. I
remember sitting in the back seat of the car going through
White Plains, New York, singing . . . "I taught the *wee-ping
wil-low* how to cry." Real slow and bluesy.

*ONSTAGE IN AMSTERDAM,
February 1972, with the
Statler Brothers. Cash's
song "A Thing Called
Love" was released
soon afterward.*

I wrote "Hey Porter" when I was
overseas. That was my homesick song
for the South. "So Doggone Lonesome" was written with Ernest Tubb
in mind. A lot of times I'd write songs
with some singer in mind, never really intending to even let them hear it,
but with them in mind. After I record-
ed "So Doggone Lonesome," Tubb heard it and did record it.

I wrote "Get Rhythm" for Elvis. But I never did let him hear
it before I recorded it. "Come In Stranger" was just my life-
on-the-road song.

*Did you give Carl Perkins the idea for "Blue Suede Shoes"?*

I remember the guys in the Air Force saying, "Don't step on
my blue suede shoes." I thought it was a good line and told Carl
he should put it into a song. But he wrote it all. It's his song.

*When you went to Columbia, you started recording in
Nashville rather than Memphis. That's when you got into the
concept albums like "Ride This Train."*

Yeah. *Ride This Train* was something I really worked on. I
think I must have had a country opera in mind without knowing it at the time. It was a kind of travelogue about the country. That was my pride. I'm still proud of that album.

*Those concept albums must have really caught people by
surprise. I don't think there were any country concept albums
before then.*

I don't think there were any, except for gospel, of course. It
was something that hadn't been done, and I got a lot of credit
for it among the other artists. A lot of other people openly
admired them, but some people didn't want to accept the fact
that a country artist was doing things like that. I had a few people tell me that it wasn't country and that it wasn't right for me
to do it. They said it wasn't commercial and all that jazz.

*How were sales?*

Well, today they sell more, for instance, than, if you'll pardon the expression, the *Fabulous Johnny Cash* album. *Ride This Train* might not have sold as many albums at first, but it sells more today. That's gratifying, that people still enjoy it.

But the memories start getting a little different when I think about an album like *The Sound of Johnny Cash*, because I remember where my head was at the time I was singing those songs. I wasn't too with-it on some of them. About '61 or '62. Songs that I did a bad job on.

"Cotton Fields." I had no business recording that song in the first place. Kind of a showbiz cotton-patch song. I mean, people made it that. Ledbetter didn't mean it that way. "Lost on the Desert." I took a good song from Billy Mize and rewrote it, and there was no need in that. Back in those times I always knew something was wrong somewhere and I'd take it out on the songs at times. I'd rewrite them. That was one of my worst albums.

*What's something else you're proud of from those days?*

One of the things I was really proud of was an EP called *The Rebel.* It contained "The Big Battle," "Remember the Alamo," "Lorena" and "The Rebel." I think that was some of my best work. "The Big Battle" was one of the first social-comment things I wrote. It was about the needless killing in war. That was in 1961. I thought it was a good record, and I still think it is. The idea being that the big battle comes after the killing . . . in the conscience, in the hearts and grief of people that suffered the loss.

*Which of the two prison albums — "Folsom" or "San Quentin" — is closer to you?*

*Folsom.* That's where I met Glenn Sherley. That's where things really started for me again. The *San Quentin* album was something I put a lot of heart into, a lot of feeling, and I'm very proud of it, but they had the television cameras going, and I was under a lot of pressure because I was right in the middle of a concert tour. I wasn't as relaxed at San Quentin. And the place is tighter anyway. There's a lot more tension at San Quentin.

*How do you feel now about your ABC television series?*

You can't believe all the problems you have with a weekly television show. You know how I love music, and when you love a song, you don't stop loving it at noon on Thursday. But that's the way it is if you're doing a weekly television show. For instance, Chris Gantry wrote a song called "Allegheny," a fantastic song. Well, the producer asks what song I want to sing on next week's show. I say I'd like to sing "Allegheny."

All right, he tells me, but we also need some old Johnny Cash songs. OK, I'll sing them, any of them, doesn't matter, I've sung them all so many times before. But as far as I'm concerned, the highlight of the show would be "Allegheny," because I loved it and I had I good arrangement worked up on it.

The next morning after the taping, you come down and the producer says, "All right, what do you want to sing now?" And I tell him, "Allegheny." He'd say, no, you can't do that, you did that last night at the taping. But I still like it. That's what I want to sing again. That's what is exciting to me at the moment. But you can't do that. It's just like all of a sudden you're a machine. You gotta cut off your head now, Cash, the head that likes "Allegheny" or "Sunday Morning Coming Down," and be somebody else. You did those songs last week. You gotta start loving something else right now.

That's the way it was. Like all of a sudden I'm a machine and everybody is pushing the buttons. I didn't like it. I wouldn't do another weekly show for anything. It might be all right to do one show a month and pick my own songs and really get into them.

I resented all the dehumanizing things that television does to you, the way it has of just sterilizing your head. So, I broke away and started going onstage with my shirttail out, enjoying myself again in the final weeks. Since then, I've done some guest shots on TV that I've enjoyed. But that's a lot different.

*Do you think about the future much?*

I just feel it as it goes. I do whatever I feel is right for me at the time. I don't try to get the jump on anybody or anything.

*Are you an optimistic person?*

Oh, yeah. I sure am. I've had seventeen years of nothing but good times as far as my music has gone. It's all been good for me. All the years have been good for me. And I see nothing but growth as far as the music business is concerned. I'm really optimistic about that, the fact that the best talents will be making it. Good talent will always be heard. There's nothing going to take the place of the human being. They can get all the Moog synthesizers that they want, but nothing will take the place of the human heart.

On the grounds *of his Old Hickory Lake home, 1969. Cash was newly married, off drugs and on a commercial and creative roll.*

OPPOSITE: JOHNNY AND June, 1971. ABOVE: *At the Mid-South Fair in Memphis in the late Sixties.*

*The*

# BALLAD

### OF

## JOHNNY & JUNE

*Their love affair inspired some of Cash's greatest music, helped him kick his drug habit and sustained them both for thirty-five years*

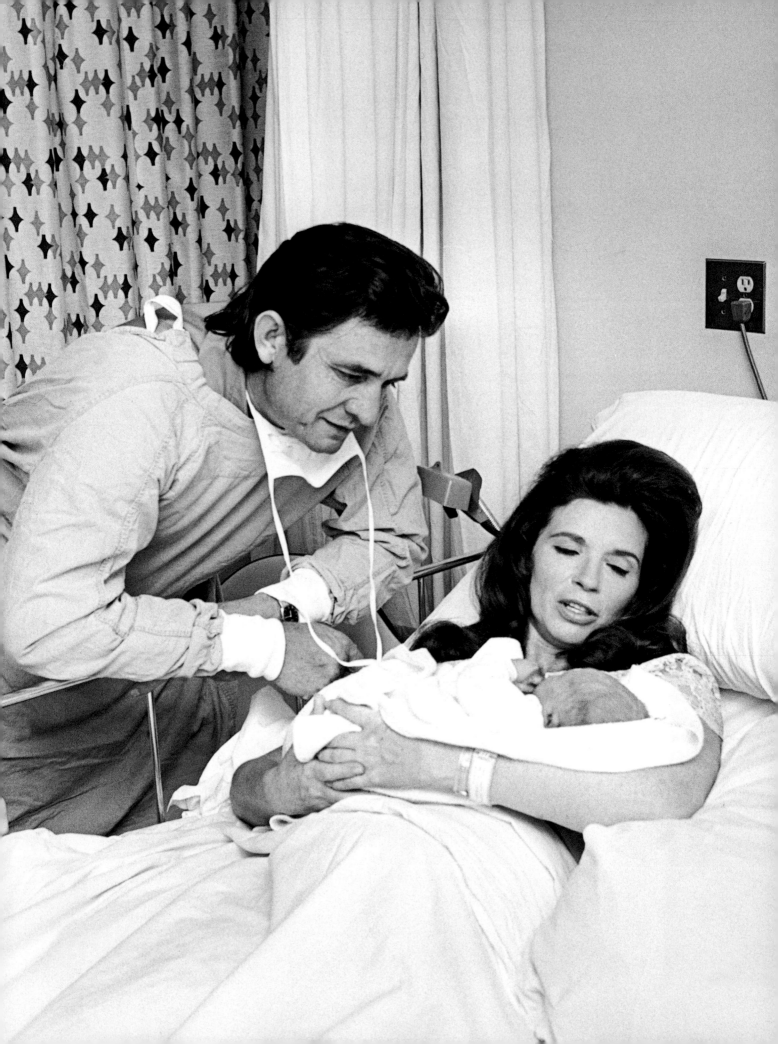

> **"I CHOSE** *to be Mrs. Johnny Cash. I decided I'd allow him to be Moses, and I'd be Moses' brother, Aaron, picking his arms up and padding along behind him."*
>
> **—JUNE CARTER CASH**

OPPOSITE: ADMIRING *their baby boy — and only child together — John Carter Cash, in March 1970.* ABOVE: *Performing together in 1975.*

FIRST LAID EYES on June Carter when I was eighteen, on a Dyess High School senior class trip to the Grand Ole Opry. I'd liked what I heard of her on the radio, and I *really* liked what I saw of her from the balcony at the Ryman Auditorium. She was great. She was gorgeous. She was a star. I was smitten, seriously so. The next time I saw her was six years later, again at the Opry, but this time backstage because by then I was a performer too. I walked over to her and came right out with it: "You and I are going to get married someday."

June is formidable; she's my solid rock. She's my spark plug. When there are people to talk to and my shyness is welling up, she holds my hand. June always sees that I've got the right thing to eat, if I'll agree to eat it. She likes the same kind of movies I do, and the same kind of TV shows.

She's got charm, she's got brains, she's got style, she's got class. She's got silver, she's got gold, she's got jewelry, she's got furniture, she's got china . . . she's got a black belt in shopping.

*From "Cash: The Autobiography"*

**"SHE'S THE GREATEST** *woman I've ever known. Nobody else, except my mother, comes close.* " **—JOHNNY CASH**

AT HOME IN HENDERSON- *ville, 1970s. "She's the easiest woman in the world for me to live with," Cash wrote in his 1997 autobiography, "because I know her so well and she knows me so well."*

**S**HE'S A VITAL PERFORMER, and it's vital for me to have her on my concerts. I just don't want to travel if she can't come with me. She almost always does. She's my life's companion, and she's a sweet companion.

She and I have become so very close, so intimate. Whenever I face a professional decision, I always put it to her because I know she'll be both objective and honest. She's never judgmental. She's become everything that a wife should be, in my mind. We sleep together, we pray together, we travel together, we work together, and we've both found our particular place where we totally belong, in every avenue of endeavor.

*From "Cash: The Autobiography"*

ABOVE: AT THEIR HOME-
away-from-home in
Jamaica, 1999. The
couple would retreat to the
island every year,
just before Christmas.
PREVIOUS PAGES: Live
in the 1970s.

THE INSPIRATION FOR
"Ring of Fire," June said,
came one morning while
she was driving her car at
4 A.M.: "I was miserable,
and I thought, 'I can't fall
in love with this man, but
it's just like a ring of fire.'"

SOUL MATES, DECEMBER
2002. "I don't want to do
anything of this world,"
Cash said after June
passed away in May
2003. "I want to make
music and do the best
work I can. That's what
she would want me to
do, and that's what I
want to do."

RS 34 • MAY 31, 1969

# JOHNNY CASH AT SAN QUENTIN

By
## RALPH J. GLEASON

*Ralph J. Gleason co-founded* ROLLING STONE *with editor Jann S. Wenner in 1967. He was one of the first real rock critics — a jazz aficionado and writer for the "San Francisco Chronicle" who also covered the burgeoning folk scene. Gleason was a contributing editor for* ROLLING STONE *until he passed away in 1975, at age fifty-eight. The following two stories originally appeared in Gleason's regular column,* Perspectives.

SPENT SIXTY DAYS in San Quentin in three hours recently, and if it hadn't been for the fact that the occasion was an appearance there of Johnny Cash, I might never have gotten out. Or so it seemed.

Let me tell you, baby, approaching the huge concrete and steel structure of San Quentin, just approaching it defines the phrase *bad vibes.*

You get the vibes in increasing intensity the closer you get to the cages and the men. *Bad vibes* is the only thing that expresses it. You can literally feel them.

It was a beautiful night. Rain in quick flashes like sudden desert storms alternated with the moon shining on the bay. San Quentin, like the ghetto at Hunters Point, has the best view ever of the bay, a touch of irony missed by most San Franciscans because they never get to either Hunters Point or San Quentin.

The moon and the huge deep purple clouds (like two-day-old bruises) were a great backdrop for the prison. You approach it on a narrow shoreline road that passes through San Quentin Village, a small country town with elm trees, a general store, half a dozen old houses with porches, and a post office and a garage laid out in a straight line to the gate of the prison.

You drive up to the gate and an elderly guard comes out.

"I'm from the *San Francisco Chronicle* and I'm supposed to attend this Cash thing tonight and my name is Gleason."

The guard looked at me, smiled and said, "You'refrom theChronicletheparkinglotisrightupthereontheleft— walkonuptotheyellowbuilding. I'msupposedtoaskyouif youhaveanyweapons."

He didn't stop for me to answer and for a minute we both chatted simultaneously as he explained where the parking lot was again and I explained that the paper bag in the front seat didn't contain a piece but a bottle of milk. I felt stupid. Who the hell takes a quart of milk to jail?

Inside—God! what a word!—there was absolutely no one visible. There was no guard. I simply walked up to the building. There were two huge battlements, with a glass-and-steel room in between, like the towers of a moat with a bridge slung between them. One said VISITORS and I went in. An old black cat shouted at me, "We closed! We closed!" I said, "Johnny Cash." And he said, "Next door."

So I went in the middle room. It was actually an enclosed tunnel between the fortress battlements, and it was full of the Cash show people, guests, a TV camera crew from Granada in England and guards.

Behind the curtains, the Carter Family (Mother Maybelle; June Carter, Johnny's old lady; and her sister) waited to go on; they were dressed like a plainer version of the King Sisters. Chicken-pie and mashed-potatoes homey. The Statler Brothers ("smokin' cigarettes and watchin' *Captain Kangaroo*"), looking like trainees at the World's Fair in unisex jackets, stood around talking to Carl Perkins, who was wearing black leather pumps rather than blue suede shoes. Perkins held his guitar firmly. He was slick and barbershop-neat and looked like a Nashville insurance salesman, but he sure could sing and play.

So the show started.

"Prison audiences are the best audiences in the world," Cash said backstage as the Statler Brothers were singing. You could tell they were by the way they applauded the Statlers. Prison life sets it up so anything at all is good in one sense. They are grateful, which is an odd emotion for an audience.

Then the Carter Family went onstage. The inmates yelled, screamed, roared and shouted. The sound when those prisoners saw the three women trot onstage was pure unadulterated lust.

✳ ✳ ✳ ✳ ✳ ✳

CASH PACED BACKSTAGE like a lion. Long strides, his gray slacks and his high-button black shoes swirling as he spun around one of the stage supports. He had on a blue open-collar shirt and his long, box-back black coat, and he sweats before he goes on. The Carter Family was onstage, and Cash gripped the curtain and yelled, HOOOEEEEY!! YEH! YEH! YEH! and the prisoners looked away from the stage to him for a minute, and then he shot across in front of the side curtain, shaking hands with the prisoners in the front row, while the cameramen followed him and a light shone down from the catwalk above, and then he leaped onstage.

Cash is electric without plugging in. His band gathers behind him and they just look like people, dressed up to go to church, maybe, but not like musicians. Cash looks like the lead in all the best TV Westerns. He's the law west of Pecos come to straighten things out, a Marshall Dillon who doesn't care what you were before, it's what you are *now* and no questions asked.

And he understands cons.

He sang 'em all his old ones. "You're bad, Johnny Cash!" an old, sour-looking con in the audience yelled, smiling. "We have cliques in here, you know," one of the guards said. "All the Okies are here tonight."

Onstage, Cash said, "I've been here three times and I feel I know how you think about some things. Some things it's none of my business what you think, and there's some things I don't give a damn *what* you think!" The cons roared their approval.

Then Cash sang a song he wrote the previous afternoon. It concerned "some of the things I feel about San Quentin."

Earlier, backstage, he said he'd written a new song for San Quentin. "It's a bloody one," he said, his smile coming out of the side of his mouth. He sings sideways like that, as if he's spent a lifetime passing the word down the line.

"San Quentin, you've been a living hell to me," Cash sang, and the audience went dead quiet. The guards looked up in the little groups they were in under the menu board hung from the ceiling, which said, "One Serving Only."

"Mr. Congressman, you don't understand," Cash sang. "What good do you think you do? Do you think I'll be different when you're through?" and the cons cheered him, "I'll leave here a wiser and a weaker man."

"San Quentin, may you rot and burn in hell," Cash screamed the last line out and then repeated it. The cons screamed back. A tall young guard spun around, smacked one fist into the other palm and said, "He's right!"

Cash sang a sacred song. Then he brought the Carter Family back. Then he and June did "Jackson" and then he did "Folsom Prison Blues" and they screamed again and then he did more religious songs.

What he did was right on the edge. If he had screwed it up one notch tighter, the joint would have exploded. He knew just when to stop.

"Cash is real," a close-cropped con told me. "These cons would spot a phony in a hot second."

The show was over, and producer Bob Johnston drawled, "I told you I didn't do nuthin' but let the tapes roll." The guests and the performers left in groups escorted by the guards, and the cons filed out the back to return to their cells. We walked across the empty courtyard and through the front gate again and showed our

*After whipping the prisoners into a near-riotous frenzy, June and Johnny take a bow.*

pass-out stamp on our left hand and the air was better even in the front yard.

The cars in the parking lot lit up and one by one they filed to the last gate, the guard stopping each one and opening the trunk to see there were no escapees hiding inside.

As I drove down the road through San Quentin Village, I realized how uptight I had been, the muscles in my stomach relaxing gradually. "What do you think of it?" the con had asked me when I told him it was my first time inside. "It's a good place to stay out of," I had remarked.

As I got out of town and back on the highway, I realized just how true that was. It is a good place to stay out of.

No wonder they are the best audiences in the world.

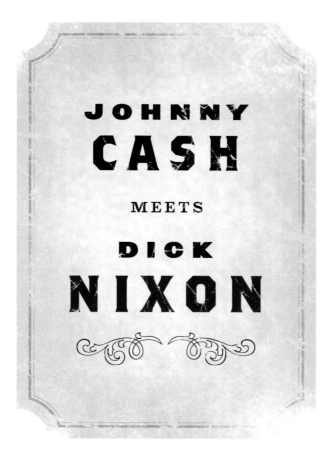

By

**RALPH J. GLEASON**

You ever look at Johnny Cash? I mean, really look? Dig those lines and that jaw and those eyes?

And that hair.

Absolutely unlike any other major artist in the country & western field, Johnny Cash has not dressed like the Texarkana version of the Pearlie Queen with fancy shirts and pants

and all the rest of the Grand Ole Opry costume.

He wears a box-back coat like some old-time line-riding preacher, a white shirt or a blue shirt and plain pants and boots.

With that hair, just long enough not to be short and too short to be hippie, he is dressed and styled in a manner that makes him acceptable to either the California Okies with all their rednecked beerbellied political conservatism and their institutional racism, or to the younger generation anywhere in the world.

It is quite an amazing thing, if you think about it. Within a year Johnny Cash had two one-hour documentaries about him shown nationally. Arthur Barron did the one for National Educational Television, the one where Bob Dylan sings with Cash in the Nashville studio and where you can see Cash walking across the Arkansas state prison yard for the only glimpse of a black face in the documentary. The other one was just shown in this country, and that's the San Quentin prison concert film.

Neither of them, curiously enough, gets anywhere near what Johnny Cash, the human being, is about. And right now the human being rather than the show business part of Johnny Cash is immensely important.

Cash's invitation to sing before Nixon crystallizes the dilemma. It's perfectly obvious that President Nixon represents the faceless, neat, mindless administrator with no sensitivity to pure humanity and no feeling for the individual.

Cash is surely the opposite: the rugged individualist, the self-sufficient man, wracked with his own torments and sensitive to those of others, seeing the inequalities of the world through his own eyes.

Cash is pure white America, part Indian, part cowboy, part sharecropper/poor man, part poet, part visionary, painfully learning how to adjust to the new facts the environment and history are insisting on, adapting his belief in God and tradition and motherhood and the rest to the growing realization of the exploitation of the society and so the racism built into it.

Now, Johnny Cash may sound somewhat less revolutionary than Dylan when he sings "What Is Truth?" but it doesn't matter. The song itself is a country & western "Times They Are a-Changin'," and there's more than one way to skin a cat. Unless we are going to divide this country into two mutually exclusive groups with the longhairs and black revolutionaries on the one side and the TV dinner/WonderBread Nixons from Muskogee on the other, we have to talk to these people. They are, after all and as difficult as it is to accept, our brothers.

No one has a better chance of talking to them than Johnny Cash. He is from their stock and their tradition and is their hero. He is now telling them long hair is not the criterion. From that position comes individuality, freedom and not a little hope. Let it go the other way long enough, and fascism will find new dimensions and repression will extend the new heights, all in the name of "Americanism."

Cash symbolizes white America, much more than the usual spokesman on the panel shows from New York or Washington. He's struggling. He's not perfect, but he's trying. He loves this country but he's trying to keep that from meaning he

During a trip to *Washington, D.C., on July 26th, 1972, Cash met with President Nixon and spoke to a Senate subcommittee about prison reform.*

hates some other, and above all he's trying to make people see that we are all in this together, there's no morality or immorality in long or short hair and dissent. I dig his humility as sincere.

The media today is matched only by the morality mix in which a thief is better morally if he has long hair than if he doesn't. There's a great number of individual traps on the road ahead and a lot of areas of danger. It is just as much a mistake to confuse long hair with a superior position as it is to confuse it with an inferior position. Every longhair ain't a good guy and every pothead ain't no prince. Good and bad don't come in those packages exclusively.

Johnny Cash doesn't apologize. He's his own man and he says what he thinks. That seems to me to be implicitly in the very way he stands onstage. It was Cash who said, "Shut up and let him sing!" when Dylan was being booed and harassed for going electric. I wasn't surprised when Cash had second thoughts about singing "Welfare Cadillac" for President Nixon. He's a strong man and a good man. He walks the line.

"THERE WAS A DIFFERENCE in the way Dad related to his family and the way he related to the public," says Cindy Cash, the third of Johnny Cash's four daughters. (The others are Rosanne, Kathy and Tara.) "A lot of people don't think of him as shy, because he was so strong. But he was a very private man. His family were really the only people he felt like he could let loose and be himself around." Cash's daughters generously contributed the photos and letters in this scrapbook. "Dad was so funny and we wanted to share that side of him," says Tara. "I

remember once we got off an elevator after a show at, like, one in the morning. There was a man sleeping in a chair with a vacuum cleaner next to him, and dad picks up the vacuum cleaner and throws it against the wall and starts running down the hall. He could be so spontaneously silly." The pages that follow document the life of a family man—taking his children on tour, writing sweet notes to them from the road, dancing at their weddings, goofing around in his backyard pool and teaching his grandkids how to fish.

WHILE CASH WAS ON TOUR IN THE EARLY EIGHTIES, HE WORE THIS SATIN JACKET *with all of his kids' names on the back and his own name on the front. "Being a dad was a big thing to him," says Cindy. Kathy adds, "If he was working, he'd take all seven of us with him. He never seemed exasperated by a bunch of kids. He loved it."*

Top: WITH TARA, ON THE GROUNDS OF HIS FARM, CIRCA 1989.
"We went out that day and shot mistletoe out of the top of the trees," Tara says. ABOVE: "That was 1976, when I was fifteen," says Tara. "We were on tour somewhere in the States. At the end of that summer was my sixteenth birthday, and Dad gave me my first car. It was an Audi Fox. I picked that because Dad was on 'Little House on the Prairie,' and we hung out with him on the set on the same stage area where they were filming 'Happy Days.' The Fonz was huge at that time, and I saw that Henry Winkler drove an Audi Fox. That's how I chose my first car."

JOHNNY CASH

TARA IS SWEET
TARA IS GOOD

WILL YOU BE
MY VALENTINE?
BOY! I WISH YOU WOULD.
Love Daddy

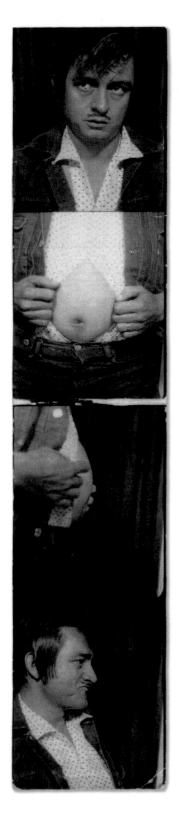

"DAD WAS MISCHIEVOUS,"
says Tara, left (at age seven).
"A lot of people didn't know
that side of him. His writings
depicted how dark the
depths of his soul ran, but
he was so funny and so
spontaneous and that's
what I loved about him."

BELOW: "THAT WAS ON
father's day," says Kathy.
"The kids were in the pool
playing, and Dad jumped
in and said, 'I wanna
ride that thing!'"

TOP LEFT: AN EARLY-SIXTIES FAN CLUB CARD.
ABOVE: *Cash when he joined the Air Force.*
LEFT: *"Mom used to always dress me and Rosanne in the same outfits," says Kathy, who is eleven months younger than her sister. "I wanted everyone to think we were twins." Here, the girls—and their baby sister, Cindy— pose with Johnny and his first wife, Vivian, for an early-Sixties photo shoot.*

"This was my grandparents' fiftieth anniversary," Tara says. "There was always a lot of singing at any type of gathering. Dad would have friends over to the house, and he and June would end up in the lakeside room having what they'd call a 'guitar pulling.'" From left: Cash's sisters Louise and Reba, his brother Roy, minister Floyd Gressett, Connie Smith, Cash's mother, Carrie (at the piano), his sister Joanne, his father, Ray, his brother Tommy and Cash himself.

At their new home in Encino, California, in the late Fifties. "We moved there when Dad started making films," says Kathy. "It was Johnny Carson's house, actually, and we rented it out. Then Dad decided he didn't like the neighborhood or being that close to Hollywood, and he found this land in Casitas Springs. He had a house built and we moved there as soon as it was finished."

"Growing up, I thought everybody's dad was on the road and musicians came and sat at your kitchen table and stayed up all night and smoked a lot of cigarettes." —KATHY

Left: SUMMER 2002, WITH ROSANNE'S SON JAKE.
*"Dad loved his typewriter," Rosanne says. "But,
being a very modern child, Jake had never seen one.
So Dad was showing him how to use it."* TOP:
*Cradling his first great-grandson, Brennan
Coggins, 1997. Brennan is Kathy's son Thomas'
first child.* ABOVE: *With Cindy and her daughter
Jessica at a school auction in 1988.*

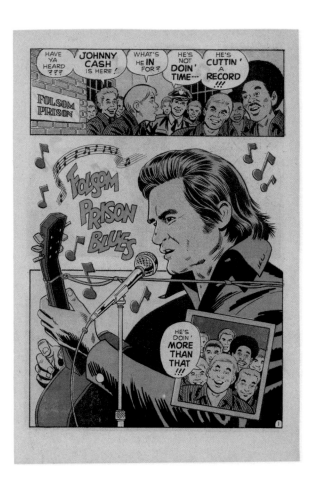

OPPOSITE: A 1976 COMIC BOOK
*produced by a Christian publish-
ing company narrated Cash's life,
from career high points such as
his Folsom Prison performance to
personal lows like drug addiction.*
LEFT: *Cash, goofing around on
the road. "He was hilarious, but
he was also a country boy, and
he could be tacky," says Cindy.*

CINDY CASH
314 8 Breaker Ct.
Ventura, Calif.

Nov 5 '74

Hi Cindy;

Mrs. Kelly just gave me
these pictures that were taken
at Anaheim.

We thought you and your
friends might like them.

Tell Tara that Mrs Kelley
is getting some together for
~~her~~ her 3rd I'll send them soon.

I'm on the bus, and it
is BUMPY.
Love
Daddy

LEFT: TARA, CINDY, KATHY and Rosanne in their Catholic school uniforms. "We had all gotten new bikes and we were getting ready to go to school," says Kathy. "We spent most of our childhood riding bikes on this huge turnaround in the driveway." BELOW: A summer outing with Dad. From left: Rosanne, Cindy, Tara, Kathy.

At Rosanne's first wedding, to country singer-songwriter Rodney Crowell, in 1979. "Dad wasn't a big dancer," Rosanne says, "but he insisted on dancing with me at the wedding. He was twirling me so hard I thought I might fall." Opposite: Cash cooling off in Hendersonville.

> "If he caught a fish, he'd talk to it while he was cleaning it. He'd tell us, 'It's saying, "Please, Johnny, please, scratch me harder."'" —TARA

AT SCHOOL WITH KATHY'S SON DUSTIN. "IN FIRST GRADE, THEY WERE *teaching the history of country music," says Kathy. "The head of the school asked me if I would get an autographed picture for Dustin's class. Dad said, 'How about if I deliver it and I'll sing them a couple of songs?' He did two or three funny songs like 'I'm Being Swallowed by a Boa Constrictor' and a couple of Christian songs. He ended up staying about an hour and a half."* OPPOSITE: *Hugging Kathy in the late Seventies. "He used to always say to each of us, 'You're my favorite.' That day, I had been kidding him about it and he just grabbed me and started 'waddling' me, as he called it."*

> **"We loved to listen to him talk, because he had such a way with words. He was wise and he was downright funny."** —CINDY

TOOLING AROUND JAMAICA IN A *golf cart: June, with John Carter on her lap, and family friend Ted Rollins in the front seat; with June's daughter Rosey Carter, Johnny and Rosanne in the back seat*

CINDY TOURED WITH HER DAD FULL-TIME FROM 1978 (WHEN SHE WAS TWENTY) TO 1983. SHE CONTINUED TO *sing with him on-and-off throughout his career. "I still felt like a daddy's girl, even in front of 10,000 people, because that's how he made me feel," she says. "He was more attentive onstage than anywhere else. I had no training as a singer; I only went on the road and sang to be with him. The times in between the concerts and sleeping where we were traveling or having a meal was when I could bond with him the best."*

OPPOSITE: TARA'S SON ALEX GAVE
*out flowers during a party Cash*
*threw at the Carter family homestead*
*in Virginia for June's 72nd birthday in*
*2001. "Dad called it Grandchildren's*
*Week," says Tara. "He sent everyone a*
*formal invitation. Everybody went—*
*thirteen grandchildren and two great-*
*grandchildren. We did a lot of singing,*
*and we took a canoe trip down the*
*Holston River in, like, ten boats."*
RIGHT: *Johnny plays guitar for*
*Rosanne's son Jake at his Jamaica*
*home in January 2000.*

ON THE GROUNDS OF THE CASH HOME
*in Tennessee. "He always took the*
*grandkids over there to fish," says*
*Kathy. "Dad loved being around kids.*
*He said, 'Kids will always tell ya like it*
*is.' He liked teaching them how to fish.*
*When we were kids and he taught me*
*and my sisters, he always said, 'You*
*always have to talk to your worm and*
*apologize to it for killing it.' He had the*
*patience of Job. He just kept rehooking*
*their lines." Tara also remembers that*
*day with the grandkids: "It was four*
*years ago, and Dad's health was really*
*starting to decline. He felt so bad that*
*day—he kept sitting down. But he*
*wouldn't complain. It was so important*
*to him to provide these experiences for*
*his grandchildren that he'd just do it."*

ABOVE: A HOLIDAY GATHERING IN HENDERSONVILLE.
*From left: Johnny, Tara, Cindy, Kathy, Rosanne. "He
used bandannas to wrap presents," says Cindy. "And for
tags, it was Post-It notes. He could have put a twenty-
four-karat ribbon on it, and it wouldn't have been more
valuable than that bandanna and that Post-It note."*
RIGHT: *Kathy's son Thomas, sporting a Johnny Cash
tour shirt in the early Seventies. Says Kathy. "He was the
first grandchild, so he would always get up and perform.
A lot of times, when the promoters would do jackets,
Dad would get little T-shirts made for the grandkids.
We've still got that one."*

# JOHNNY CASH

February 9, 1972

Dear Cindy,

I don't have my tour schedule for this year yet, but as soon as
Saul gets it to me, I will send it to you.

I do know that I am playing a tour in New England in April.
Some of the dates are New York City, Boston, and Hartford,
Connecticut, but I don't know the exact dates yet.  I will let
you know as soon as I find out.

It seems to me though that you must improve your school grades.
Do you reckon the fact that you got a bad grade in conduct had
something to do with the other bad grades?  You must pay
attention in class and be a young lady.

Be sweet — I love you,

*Daddy*

HI TARA!
HI TARA!
HOW ARE
YOU? I LOVE
YOU, DADDY

HI DADDY
I ALWAYS
ZIP CODE

Post Card
I

MISS TARA CASH
P.O. BOX 44
CASITAS SPINGS
CALIF.

ABOVE: "THAT FACE HE'S MAKING," SAYS
Kathy, "we would call his 'You're gonna
do what?' face. That was such a Dad
thing: When he got that face, you knew
you'd better explain." Tara adds, "Then,
after you told him, he would always
follow up with, 'Well, all right.'"
RIGHT: Cash's parents, Ray and Carrie,
with Rosanne's daughter Caitlin at their
sixtieth anniversary party in 1980.
OPPOSITE: In the summer of 1967,
Cash's daughters went from Los Angeles
to his new home in Hendersonville for the
first time since he and Vivian divorced.
"He used to have an apartment with
Waylon [Jennings]," says Kathy, "but
Mom wouldn't let us visit him there."

July '74

Cindy;
Keep the smile upon your face
Keep things in order and in place
Keep your values within sight
Know for sure whats wrong and right

Write a new song every day
To keep you singing on your way
Sing with all your heart and mind
You'll be a joy to humankind.

Much Love
Daddy

Left: "i kept every letter he sent me," says Cindy. "We heard from him most of the time by telephone, but he liked to write letters, and he would get on the plane or a bus and write letters to pass the time. The oldest letter I have is from 1964. It ends with, 'Tell Mama I love her.' The letters were everything to me when we didn't live together and before I became an adult. By keeping Dad's letters, I got to keep a part of him that no one else got." Below: With Cindy (left) and Tara, in the early Eighties. Opposite: The girls visit with their dad and baby half-brother John Carter at the Beverly Hills Hotel in the early Seventies. From left: Tara, Cindy, Johnny, John, Rosanne, Kathy.

**BROKEN DOWN** *in* **BRANSON**

Highway 76, the main drag in Branson, Missouri, cuts a gaudy swath through a landscape that was once beautiful mountain country. Block after block is made up of cut-rate motels, miniature golf courses, water slides, chain restaurants — and theaters that showcase the work of

*By* **STEVE POND**

fading country stars, showbizzy pop singers, Japanese fiddle players and, occasionally, a genuine American legend.

On a chilly day in the spring of 1992, one of those legends sat in the back seat of a black Ford Explorer as it traveled down Highway 76 at twilight. "Many of my

*"I'm gonna use my old simple sound and hope to come up with something." Cash said in 1992 — two years before his comeback.*

friends came here and built theaters, and they liked it," Johnny Cash said as he looked out the window. "I thought, 'I'll never do that. I'll just keep hittin' the road until I'm too old to bop, and then I'll drop.'"

But by the early 1990s, things had changed for Cash. More than a decade since his last Top Ten song on the country charts — and sixteen years since he'd had a mainstream pop hit — the career of the sixty-year-old Man in Black was at an all-time low point. He was still lauded for his past — a new box set documented his work from 1955 to 1983, while two months

earlier he'd been inducted into the Rock & Roll Hall of Fame. But his future, he thought, might be spent in Branson. The town, nestled in the Ozark Mountains just north of Cash's home state of Arkansas, was Las Vegas without slot machines or strippers, a place where busloads of Middle American tourists came to fish, camp and watch performers like Andy Williams, Mel Tillis, Tony Orlando and Boxcar Willie. "I don't know," Cash said slowly. "It's a place where folks can come, and I can settle down and do what I like without having to hit the road." He paused. "I feel good about it." He sounded as if he were trying to convince himself as much as anyone else. What he didn't know was that the backer who was financing his Cash Country Theatre was about to run out of money; the lavish white building with two stages and a massive Frederic Remington bronze in its rotunda would never open to the public. Within a couple of months, Cash would be back on the road, on the run from a recurring addiction to pain pills and on the verge of a historic renaissance with Rick Rubin's American Recordings label.

At the moment, though, he and his wife, June Carter Cash, figured they'd be spending a lot of time in Branson. This meant they needed supplies — which brought them to Highway 76, and to the huge Wal-Mart store that sat near

a curve in the road. Inside the store, Johnny pushed a shopping cart through the men's department, while June steered her own cart to another part of the store. Scanning the racks, Cash pulled out two pairs of shiny warm-up pants — one black, the other medium blue — and put them in his cart. He added eight pairs of black socks, walked around the department for a few more minutes, then stopped and pulled the blue pants out of his cart. "I don't know," he said slowly, frowning as he held them up. "Do you think these look a little fruity?"

Without waiting for an answer, he put them back on the rack and headed for the cashier, his cart filled with nothing but black. Along the way, he left a wake of incredulous shoppers. "Hello, how are you?" nodded Cash to everyone who showed a glint of recognition — which is to say, everyone he passed.

To the Wal-Mart shoppers, it didn't matter much that they hadn't heard a new song by Johnny Cash on the radio in years. But Cash was feeling it. He'd left Columbia Records in 1986 after twenty-eight years on the label, feeling that the company had lost interest and his work had suffered. He signed with Mercury, for whom he'd made five albums, from *Johnny Cash Is Coming to Town* in 1987 to *The Mystery of Life* four years later. Sprinkled throughout the albums were terrific songs, among them the Elvis Costello tunes "Hidden Shame" and "The Big Light," Guy Clark's elegiac "Let Him Roll" and Cash's tough, apocalyptic "Goin' by the Book." But the albums didn't sell, and Cash was fed up with what he felt was a lack of support from the record company. "They have a right to option one more album," he said as he waited for June at the Wal-Mart snack bar. "But I'm probably gonna tell them that I'm not interested in staying with 'em."

Still, he had plans. Cash talked about recording intimate albums, rockabilly albums, gospel albums, about revisiting old songs and trying out new ones like Dire Straits' "Walk of Life." "My new stuff is going to be real sparse," he added. "Never more than four instruments in the studio at any one time. I'm gonna keep it real clean and bare, use today's technology with my old simple sound, and hope to come up with something."

The day after shopping at Wal-Mart, Johnny and June took a limo to Springfield, about an hour north of Branson, to do a series of radio interviews and also sign autographs at a massive convention of fishermen and fishing equipment. On the way to Springfield, June did most of the talking, while Cash sat in the back of the limo rubbing his jaw.

The story she told was a horrific one, a tale of botched dental work, a fractured jaw, attempted remedies that went wrong. "Until six months ago, we thought John might lose the jaw," she said. "Now he's got a platinum plate in there, and it's holding, but he's in a lot of pain." She looked at her husband. "I said to him, 'Why does it always happen to you?' And he said, 'Thank God at least it happened to somebody who can take it.'"

By the time he finished signing two hours' worth of autographs at the fishing convention, Cash was exhausted, his hands shook slightly, and his jaw was beginning to swell. He reached into his pocket and pulled out a prescription bottle. "You don't have to put this in the article," he said, downing two pills.

Gamely, Cash sat for two interviews at a local radio station, both of them concerned far more with his past than his future. One deejay, curiously, kept asking about a time Cash and Elvis supposedly swapped shirts while performing on *Louisiana Hayride.* "I couldn't switch shirts with Elvis," said Cash, confused. "I'm bigger than Elvis."

Afterwards, the deejay asked Cash to record a message for his answering machine, then requested an autograph as well. "I bet you don't remember the first time I met you," he said as Cash was leaving. "It was 1966, and you were in pretty bad shape."

"Yeah," said June with a knowing smile, "he coulda been."

"You, too," said the deejay to June. "In fact, Johnny, we were taking bets on how long you'd be alive, and the longest anybody would bet on was two years."

In the car, Cash was steaming. "What was all that stuff about me and Elvis switching shirts?" he snapped. "That didn't make any sense, but he just kept talking about it. That's the stupidest thing I ever heard."

"That was weird," agreed June. "He was sayin' *I* was in bad shape, too? What did he mean by that? I was *never . . .*"

"No," agreed Johnny, "you never were."

Cash was supposed to stop at another radio station for two more interviews, but the schedule had left him drained; since bypass surgery four years earlier, he was used to taking a nap every afternoon. "I don't know if I can do any more," he said, sighing as he reached for his pain pills.

"The problem is," said June, "if you cancel anything, the stories are gonna have you in the hospital before the end of the day."

Cash considered canceling both interviews, or doing one but canceling the other. Suddenly, though, he sat up straight and announced, "*No.* I'll do them both." His tone was hard, abrupt—a *fuck you* tone of voice aimed not at anyone in the limousine but at the demands of being Johnny Cash around the clock.

At the radio station, Cash was out of the car and into the building before the driver could turn off the ignition. An hour later, he returned to the limo and slumped into his seat. "That was a nightmare," he moaned. "Every time I thought we were finished, they said, 'just two more things.' But we got it *done.*" He was weak and in pain, but for the moment Johnny Cash was also proud, defiant and maybe even a bit triumphant.

"You know, I'm doing what I feel like I was put on this world to do," he said, fighting through the hurt and the fatigue, the years of neglect and disinterest. "I just want to do more of the same, but I want to do it better. I want to make some records that people will pay attention to, you know?"

# THE ROLLING STONE INTERVIEW

*By*

**STEVE POND**

Keith Richards didn't have it. Neither did Neil Young, Jeff Beck, Jimmy Page, John Fogerty, Robbie Robertson or the Edge. They'd all gathered at the Rock & Roll Hall of Fame induction ceremony last January, but none of them had the authority or magnetism of the tall, weathered Man in Black. On a night designed to celebrate rock & rollers, country singer Johnny Cash was clearly the coolest man in the room.

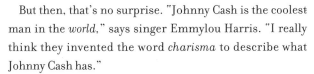

But then, that's no surprise. "Johnny Cash is the coolest man in the *world*," says singer Emmylou Harris. "I really think they invented the word *charisma* to describe what Johnny Cash has."

Others agree. "I would rather spend a day with Johnny Cash than a week with any up-and-coming pop star," said Bono a few years ago. Bruce Springsteen says he listened incessantly to Cash's Sun recordings in the days before he wrote his album *Nebraska*, a work haunted by the spare, doomy sound of Cash's record. Cash later recorded two *Nebraska* tunes himself.

Cash still tours incessantly with June and their son John Carter Cash, and people come to see him not because of his last album but because he delivers, because he exudes honesty and integrity, because he's a monument to a certain kind of American spirit. They come because he is Johnny Cash.

*I hear you had an encounter with Keith Richards in the men's room before the Rock & Roll Hall of Fame ceremony.*

Yeah. I was standing at the urinal, and Keith Richards walked in and stood behind me and started singing "Loading Coal," from the *Ride This Train* album. And then he said, "Look at this. I'm takin' a piss with Johnny Cash. We need a picture of this." I said, "No, Keith, we *don't* need a picture of this."

*The next day, didn't you go on "Sesame Street"?*

Yeah. I really would like to do *Sesame Street* about once every six months. And now they've got a new character called Ronnie Trash. They were gonna call him Johnny Trash, but they decided they'd change it to Ronnie. He dresses in black, and everywhere he goes he cleans up trash.

*From taking a piss with Keith Richards to appearing alongside Big Bird, you certainly cross lots of boundaries.*

Well, I never did like musical bags or categories, you know? We busted out on our own at Sun Records in the Fifties, with our long hair and sideburns and black clothes, and they called us every name under the sun, from "rockabilly" to "white nigger." I took it with pride, because they were telling me, "You're different." I didn't set out to sound different from everybody else, but when I realized that I was different, then I was thrilled to death.

CASH HAD BEEN OUT OF *the spotlight when he was inducted into the* Rock & Roll Hall of Fame *in 1992.* PREVIOUS PAGE: *Emerging from the darkness, 1994.*

WITH MINNIE PEARL, *one of his first Nashville supporters, in the Fifties*

*But you had real trouble at the Grand Ole Opry.*

Yeah, I had my second record out. It was a hit on every kind of radio station. My manager said, "You know, the Grand Ole Opry's the ultimate." So he took me up there, and I wore my black shirt and pants and my short boots, not cowboy boots. And I sat for two hours in the manager's office. Finally he looked at me and said, "What makes you think you belong on the Grand Ole Opry?" I said, "Well, I got a record that is in the best sellers now, and I think those people would like to hear me sing it." And he said, "OK, be here Saturday night." He didn't ask me, he told me. I did "Cry, Cry, Cry," and then I did "Hey Porter," and it turned out I encored seven times.

A lotta people supported me coming to Nashville: Ernest Tubb, Hank Snow, Minnie Pearl. . . . And then there were some who would make it a point to let me hear the remarks they were saying as I walked by. It was the same thing they were calling Elvis: "white nigger." And you know, when I left that night, I said, "I don't wanna go back to this place anymore. I don't have to put up with that crap."

*What shows impressed you when you started listening to music?*

There was a hillbilly show on WMPS radio that was really popular, with Eddie Hill and the Louvin Brothers, Ira and Charlie Louvin. The show was called *The High Noon Roundup.* It went on from 12:00 to 12:30, and at 1:00 *The Lonesome Valley Trio* came on, which was Eddie Hill and the Louvin Brothers singing gospel songs. I was working in the cotton fields, and I used to beg my daddy to let me stay at the house until 1:15, when *The Lonesome Valley Trio* was over. I went to Memphis when I was fourteen to see that show. And the thrill of my life was sitting in the front row, and before the show started, Eddie Hill walked out and said, "You got a request?" I said, "Yeah, I sure do. Could you dedicate a song to my mother on the *Lonesome Valley Trio* show?" So Eddie Hill and the Louvin Brothers sang a song called "I'll Have a New Life" for my mother.

*Onstage you talk about a black shoeshiner in Memphis inspiring "Get Rhythm." Didn't you write that for Elvis?*

Uh-huh. Sam wouldn't let him have it, though. And I guess Elvis forgot about it, or he would have called and asked me for it.

*Did you stay in touch with Elvis after he left Sun?*

No. I saw him a few times. See, I moved to California in '58, and I saw Elvis once in a while when he was there shooting a movie. The last time I saw him was when he was doing *G.I. Blues.* He had rented the top floor of the Beverly Wilshire Hotel, and I was up there with him watching that bunch of moochers that hung after him. I mean, he fed a lot of people.

I saw Elvis closing his little world around him — out of necessity, he had to — and so I stayed away, hoping everyone else would. The last thing he needed was another mooch or somebody else trying to sap his energy and take his time, like so many of them did.

*You've said you wrote "Folsom Prison Blues" after seeing a television documentary about that prison. But how about that famous line "I shot a man in Reno/Just to watch him die"? Did you get that from the show?*

No, that was from my head. It was a violent movie, and I just wanted to write a song that would tell what I thought it would be like to be in prison. Merle Haggard came up with a great line after I had those prison hits and after he got out

ILLUSTRATION BY JON LANGFORD

of prison. He said, "Johnny Cash understands what it's like to be in prison, but he doesn't *know*."

*Your own experiences in jail were all brief.*

Overnight, yeah. I was thrown in jail seven times, and I got treated rough twice by guards who slammed me against the wall and beat me in the kidneys. One of them knocked me out. One was in Carson City, Nevada, and one was El Paso.

*You'd been making some pretty adventurous albums for Columbia, but then in the mid-Sixties you put out the album "Everybody Loves a Nut," and your music got a lot sillier.*

I think that came out of amphetamines. It was part of my craziness at that time, and it happened to find its way onto the tape. I mean, I thought some of those songs were funny. And I thought it might show that I did have a sense of humor. But there were no great songs on that album, that's for sure.

*Have you ever felt free of the addiction?*

I never crave 'em anymore. I haven't had amphetamines in ten years. I never think about them. I think amphetamines would kill me if I got back on 'em. I've had to take a lot of pain medication for the broken jaw, but that's all.

*Are you proud of your work on Columbia during the Seventies and early Eighties, or do you think it got off track?*

It got off track, yeah. There were times when I didn't care. It was, like, complete apathy from the record company, and I guess I got that way too. Finally, we both agreed that we weren't entertaining each other anymore. When they said, "Let's start talking about renewing the contract," I said, "Let's face it, nobody down here wants me. Nobody's interested in producing me or trying to sell my records. I'll go somewhere else, thank you very much."

*Do you own the rights to your old songs now?*

Yeah. When I had bypass surgery in '88, I sold the company because we needed the money. And then I fought to get that company back. I got every song back, and I'll never give it up again. I don't give a shit what happens financially, I'll never give up my songs again.

*You left Columbia after twenty-five years, but your career didn't take off at Mercury.*

Nobody at that company is excited about my recording career. If I hear "demographics" one more time, I'm gonna puke right in their faces. I mean, I recorded songs that I think are really some of my best work, like the last album, *The Mystery of Life*, but I think they must have pressed a hundred copies and sent 'em out. I don't know. They're ex-

cited about Kathy Mattea and the other young artists. Which is all right. I was there once. But they're gonna be old someday. And the thing is, if you got it, you always got it, you know?

*There's a line in "I'm Gonna Sit on the Porch and Pick on My Old Guitar" that goes, "Pleasing everybody but me is my first goal." Is that what you've done?*

Yeah, I feel like that's what my life's all about half the time. And I've just about had it with that. I want to please me.

*Do you have an idea of how you want to please yourself?*

Not really. I wanna do an album called *Johnny Cash: The Rockabilly Years*. I'd like to do another concept album – but even more in-depth – about the culture and the religion and the things that we're losing by the Native American being assimilated into the white man's world. And I'd like to do an album called *Johnny Cash: Late and Alone*. I'd like to do really hard songs and gut songs and say things that you don't hear these days. I mean, sing intimate, really intimate to that woman, you know? Things that my fans would be surprised to hear me say.

*"The thing is, if you got it, you always got it," said Cash, pictured here with Rosanne at her wedding to producer-musician John Leventhal in 1995.*

*Do you miss the days when people paid closer attention to what you had to say?*

Well, I guess I'd be lying if I said I didn't. Yeah, I do. But I don't grieve over it. I mean, hell, I don't lose sleep over not having a record in the charts. But I know that I'm capable of doing a lot better work than I've been doing the last few years, and I want to get into a situation where I can do that.

*But can you continue to play as many shows as you do and make these new records that you want to make? I mean, things like a broken jaw can take their toll.*

Ah, that don't mean nothin'. Drive on. [*Laughs*] That's from a book I've been reading about Vietnam. It's called *The 13th Valley*, by John Del Vecchio. There are all these great expressions that men had in Vietnam, and one of them is "Screw it. Don't mean nothing. Drive on." Meaning, if it isn't life-threatening, don't worry about it. Since I had my sixtieth birthday, I've been using that expression a lot. I'm trying to learn that I can't sweat the little things the way I used to do. So what if I've got a broken jaw? It could be worse. Could be a broken back. Screw it. It don't mean nothing. Drive on.

# RICK RUBIN

### THE

# ROLLING STONE

### INTERVIEW

### By

# DAVID FRICKE

"HE WAS REAL EXCITED," Rick Rubin recalled, describing his last phone conversation with Johnny Cash, on September 11th, 2003. "I said, 'We finished all the mixes, and we're sending them to you this weekend, so you can hear them all.' " They were discussing the imminent completion of *Unearthed*, a box set of previously unissued songs and alternate takes from the sessions for the four albums Cash had made in the past decade, all produced by Rubin and issued to cross-generational acclaim on Rubin's American label: *American Recordings* (1994), *Unchained* (1996), *American III: Solitary Man* (2000) and *American IV: The Man Comes Around* (2002).

Cash never heard those mixes. He died the next day in a Nashville hospital at the age of seventy-one. It was the end of an extraordinary and monumental life, a chapter unto itself in the history of American song. But his passing also brought to a conclusion an enduring and defiantly successful friendship: the baritone patriarch of country music and the much younger rap and metal iconoclast; the Man in Black and the man behind the board for, among many others, Run-DMC, the Beastie Boys, Slayer and the Red Hot Chili Peppers.

CASH AND RUBIN working on "Unchained" – Cash's second American Recordings album – in a California studio in 1996

Johnny Cash and Rick Rubin were born three decades and several worlds apart: Cash in 1932, in Kingsland, Arkansas, to struggling cotton-farmer parents; Rubin into suburban prosperity on Long Island, New York, in 1963, the year Cash scored his Number One hit "Ring of Fire." And when they met for the first time, backstage after a Cash show in Orange County, California, in 1993, their careers were at opposite poles. Rubin was coming off his first multi-platinum decade as a producer; an original co-founder of Def Jam Records, a hip-hop institution; and the head of his own eclectic American imprint. Cash was labelless, cast aside by the Nashville establishment after nearly forty years of making historically vital albums and hit singles for Sun, Columbia and Mercury Records.

But together, Cash and Rubin created a body of work that artistically and commercially transformed Cash's sunset years as a country star. Rubin recorded the undiminished subterranean force of Cash's voice with haunting clarity, in small-combo and hearthside-solo settings that combined the sepia atmosphere of a nineteenth-century daguer-rotype and the fire-when-ready immediacy of Cash's Sun sessions. Rubin also introduced the man who wrote "Folsom Prison Blues" and "I Walk the Line" to the melodies and lyrics of a new daredevil generation of songwriters, including Beck, Nick Cave and Trent Reznor of Nine Inch Nails. Emboldened by Rubin's faith in him and his future, Cash sang those songs — as well as traditional favorites, treasured hymns and fresh originals — with old-warrior authority and fearless honesty.

TOM PETTY AND THE Heartbreakers backed Cash on "Unchained," which included covers of Soundgarden's "Rusty Cage" and Beck's "Rowboat."

"The connection we made didn't seem to come from the words we spoke," Rubin said of that initial backstage encounter, in the first of two extensive interviews conducted in the weeks after Cash's death. Rubin actually described that empathy as "a feeling of safety" — and it went both ways. "Johnny was made fun of in Nashville for working with me," Rubin noted. "It seemed ridiculous to that audience. But he saw the seriousness of what we talked about and could do together — enough to go against those feelings."

Here is an intimate, detailed account of how far Cash dared to go in his final, triumphant years — from the man

who walked the line with him, to the end.

*What are your earliest memories of Johnny Cash and his music? Until you started producing his records, you were best known for working with rap and heavy metal acts.*

Johnny was a figure in my life when I was growing up, an icon who was always there. I saw him on TV – I remember seeing him on an episode of *Columbo* – and he just seemed like an interesting person. I wasn't a die-hard fan collecting his records. I liked more extreme things then.

*Did your experiences in rap and metal – genres characterized by violent narrative and intense self-examination – influence your vision of Johnny as an artist, of what he had yet to achieve on record?*

I never thought about that. It's possible. But before I worked with him, the most famous line in any song he sang was "I shot a man in Reno/Just to watch him die." It's a piece of his mythology. Of course, he was more rounded than that. But as a producer, I focused on finding what was unique to Johnny and amplifying that: "What is a song that he could sing, that James Taylor couldn't sing? And why is that?"

*This was a man who had worked with Sam Phillips at Sun Records and many of the top producers in Nashville. What do you think he saw in you as a record maker?*

I will tell you something that someone told me at the funeral. A friend of his said that he just wanted to let me know how much Johnny cared about me. Johnny told him, "Rick saw something in me that I didn't know was there anymore. Because of that, when the work we did was accepted, it made me trust him."

> "AS A PRODUCER,
> I focused on finding
> what was unique to
> Johnny and amplifying
> that," says Rubin.

He was not an ego-driven person. He did not come from a place of confidence. For all of his success, he was somewhat insecure.

*It's hard to imagine a man of such titanic presence and voice being unsure of himself.*

For the first album, we tried a lot of experiments – recorded with bands, did all kinds of things – to find out what this new sound was going to be, before we went back to the acoustic recordings he did in my living room, the style of the earliest demos we'd done. Then I asked him if he would get up at a club and do a set of acoustic material. I felt it would have an impact on the recording we were doing. We set up a show at the Viper Room [in Los Angeles]. And he was terrified before going on. This was a guy who did 200 shows a year for forty years – he'd played prisons – and the idea of going up by himself and singing songs absolutely terrified him. I remember how nervous he was through the first song. Then everyone accepted him. By the end of the second song, he was fine. [The live versions of "Tennessee Stud" and "The Man Who Couldn't Cry" on *American Recordings* come from that night.]

I'll tell you another interesting story. In 2003, he got a lifetime achievement award from Country Music Television. He was planning on going to the ceremony, and I went to Nashville to accompany him. He ended up not feeling well enough to go, so I watched it on television with him. He was in a wheelchair; he couldn't see very well. He was really suffering.

At one point, I asked him, "What's going on? What have you been thinking about?" He said, "I've been working on saying 'I' and 'me' less. Six or seven years ago, I sent you one of my new songs. We talked about it, and you said, 'Do you think we could take out some of the I's and me's?' You don't know how deeply I took that. I've been thinking about it and working on it ever since that day."

It was so unbelievable. He was someone who really strived to be the best he could at all times. Clearly, if you look at his history, he didn't always succeed. His life was like a tug of war. But for the time I was with him, his last ten years or so, he was on the winning side of the rope.

*What kind of conversations would you have with Johnny – about songs and approach – before starting work on an album?*

It was about songs. That was the key to everything – talking about songs, how to best get him across in those songs, then feeling like he engulfed and owned them. He knew when he liked something. And if an experiment didn't work, he would let me know. He was always nice about it. He would say, "What do you think about this one?" If I said I loved it, he would be open to continuing. But if I said, "Hmm, I don't know," he would say, "Well, I don't like it either."

*Describe an actual session. Did he have to work his way up to a master take, or was he always ready?*

He was always ready, unless he wasn't feeling right, health-wise – if he was having trouble breathing. Also, he did better with the phrasing in traditional songs than in modern-written songs. A complicated, intellectually writ-

ten song like "Bridge Over Troubled Water," by Simon and Garfunkel [on *The Man Comes Around*], was difficult for him. It had more to do with structure. Beck wrote a modern song, "Rowboat" [on *Unchained*], but it's in a traditional style, so it was easy for Johnny to sing.

*How did you sell him on Trent Reznor's "Hurt"?*

He just heard the words. They resonated with him. When I sent it to him, I said, "I really feel like this one has the potential to be special." I don't know if he would have picked it, but I asked him to listen closely to the words. I imagined him singing it and knew how powerful it could be.

*Did you have to explain to him who these younger writers were?*

Always. When Joe Strummer came to visit, Johnny didn't know who he was. He'd heard of the Clash but wasn't familiar with their music. When I played him their cover of "I Fought the Law," he said, "I always wanted to record that song."

He was open to new things. If you go back to his second wave of popularity, when he had his TV show in the late Sixties and Seventies, he would feature the songwriters of the day – Neil Young, Neil Diamond, Bob Dylan. He felt an empathy for the music of the moment. On *The Man Comes Around*, he brought in the Sting song "I Hung My Head." But he also wanted to do Stephen Foster songs. If he liked a song, it didn't matter who sang it before. It was one of the jokes he would tell: "No song out there is safe."

*After "Unchained" won the Grammy for Best Country Album in 1997, you ran an ad in "Billboard" with that classic Jim Marshall photo of Johnny practically shoving his fist – middle finger outstretched – into the camera. Was that your response to the lack of support from the mainstream country industry – or his?*

That was my idea. He laughed and said, "I'm not gonna tell you not to do it." I won't say he didn't have reservations [*laughs*]. But here was a guy who had helped to build country music, saw that industry turn its back on him – and then he wins the most coveted Grammy in country music, with no one lifting a finger in the Nashville community. It was the recognition that he knew he deserved.

*Did the success of "American Recordings" give you the license to be even more extreme in the choice of songs on later albums?*

One of the most extreme songs that I brought to him was "The Mercy Seat," by Nick Cave, which he did on *American III*.

He loved it. As a matter of fact, there was a bit of an argument when we were sequencing the album. He wanted it to be the first song. I thought it would scare everybody [*laughs*]. What can you play after it? You couldn't hold people's attention with a regular song. He had to build up to it.

*Did you ever suggest that he cover a rap or hip-hop song?*

No. It's not who he was. I suggested "Hurt," because I could imagine Johnny Cash singing those words. When he sings them, you think he could have written them. One problem was that some songs had baggage, like "Desperado." You've heard the Eagles sing it forever. That took it away from Johnny in my eyes. But he suggested it, and he did a great job.

*His health first took a turn for the worse while you were making "Unchained." In the cover photo, he looks much older and weakened than he did on the front of "American Recordings." What was his physical and emotional state at the time?*

The sessions were fun, because Tom Petty and the Heartbreakers were there, and they loved Johnny so much. But it was the first time we had seen him not feeling well, where he had to lie down on a couch for a while before he could sing again. But if there was a bad day, we would circle back to the material a couple of days later and get a great take.

Some of the tracks now on the box set are things that we liked the idea of, but when we actually recorded them, we thought, "Hmm, this isn't going to work." There was a Dolly Parton song, "I'm a Drifter" [from her 1976 album *All I Can Do*]. We tried it for the first album and the second album. One version was recorded with Tom Petty and the Heartbreakers, one with, I think, the Red Hot Chili Peppers' rhythm section. They're both good, but neither of them felt up to what was on the rest of those albums.

*By the time of "The Man Comes Around," there was a poignant fragility to his singing, compared to the defiant strength in his voice on "Unchained." Was there a sense that the fourth album could be his last?*

*Unchained* was hard to make, because that was right when he got sick. His body was still quite strong, but his psyche was confused, because he didn't know what was hitting him. On *The Man Comes Around*, his body was weaker, but his psyche was stronger. He knew what was going on; he was more in control.

On the other hand, he wanted "We'll Meet Again" to be the last song on that record. He had all of the people around –

his staff in Nashville, the people who worked on the record and in his home – sing along on "We'll Meet Again." When we came to L.A. to finish the record, he said to me, "You have to sing on it." All of the guitar players in L.A. who were on the album: "You guys have to sing on it too. I want everybody on this." He was adamant about it.

*And yet the two of you did a considerable amount of recording for a fifth album in the months before his death.*

He had lost the ability to walk. He was having more trouble enjoying anything, doing anything. Then June passed away. He had suffered a lot of pain in his life, but this was by far the worst he'd ever had to deal with. But a strange thing happened. He became more driven about work. He booked a session for three days after June passed. He said, "I don't want to do any of the things some people do when they lose their partner. I don't want to spend a lot of money and meet a lot of girls. I don't want to do anything of this world. I want to make music and do the best work I can. That's what she would want me to do, and that's what I want to do."

Some days, he'd book a session and he wouldn't be well enough to sing. Other days, he would do three or four days of singing, then take a couple of days to rest. In Nashville, we usually recorded in this log cabin, on a nature preserve across the street from his home. When he was too ill to leave the house, we moved the equipment there. The last session we did in Nashville was in one of the bedrooms. We did a bunch of songs in a few days. I extended my stay because we were on a roll. But he ended up going back into the hospital.

*Do you still think of songs for him to sing? And is there a particular number, something special, that you now wish you had recorded before he died?*

I think of songs for him all the time. There was one that we were planning to do for the next album, that we hadn't gotten to yet, and I'm sick about it – "A Place in the Sun," by Stevie Wonder. I envisioned that as the greatest Johnny Cash song ever. I played it for him, and he was down for doing it when he got to California. But he died the week before he was going to come.

I still make notes when I hear songs for him to sing. Because I'm not gonna stop. There was one that I heard the other day. I'd never heard it before, and I only heard half of it. I'm torn – should I track this song down, listen to it and feel bad? Probably so.

# MR. COOL

By **JANCEE DUNN**

Can you name anyone in this day and age who is as cool as Johnny Cash? No, you can't. He's the genuine article, the real deal, and he was a badass long before most of today's young whelps were born. Cash is feeling mighty good these days, what with an instant classic of an album, *American Recordings*, produced by Rick Rubin and recorded in both Cash's own cabin in Hendersonville, Tennessee, and Rubin's Hollywood living room. There is also a renewed, almost frenzied interest in the man. Hipsters, actors and models clog his shows in the vain hope that some of the Cash mystique will rub off on them. Cash takes all this attention with his usual calm as he chats from his hotel room at Los Angeles' Four Seasons Hotel, where he's registered under his own damn name. "What name would I be under?" he booms. "I mean, who cares?"

*I just can't picture you staying in swanky hotels like the Four Seasons.*

Well, where would I stay?

*I don't know, I guess . . .*

I don't know anybody here in L.A. that I would want to stay with. And hotels are my life. Plus, I like room service.

*Now, you said you discovered a whole new world of music this year. How so?*

Well, really what I discovered, I guess, is myself. I discovered my own self and what makes me tick musically and what I really like. It was really a great inward journey, doing all these sessions over a period of nine months and Rick sitting there not so much as a producer but as a friend who shared the songs with me. "What else you got?" he'd say, or "Listen to this one," and he'd play one.

*You recorded seventy songs. What will become of the ones you didn't use?*

I think a lot of them will be used, and I'm not sure how. A lot of them are songs of the ilk that are on the album, some of them have other instruments on them. A few sparse instruments. A lot of them are just me and my guitar. I always wanted to do an album of gospel songs like that, you know. And Rick kinda liked some of 'em, so we may do that, too.

*Could you describe your first encounter with Glenn Danzig?*

You mean my one encounter with Glenn Danzig? Well, I went into Rick's house one night, and he was sitting here with this young man, and Rick said, "This is Glenn. Glenn has a song for you, John." So I sat down opposite him with a guitar, and he started singing this song, "Thirteen." He sang it over four or five times, then I started singing it with him, and then I sat down and recorded it. And it was

only after I got through that I knew who he was. I'd heard of the group Danzig, but Rick didn't say, "Glenn Danzig," he said, "Glenn."

*I once read that Rick wasn't incredibly familiar with your music but that he thought you were cool. How do you feel about that?*

Well, I appreciate him thinkin' I'm cool. I didn't expect him to be all that familiar with my music. I gave him the big box set, and I gave him my discography that goes back to '55.

*So he studied up a bit?*

Well, really, it was in case he wanted to know anything about me or my recordings. But we sat down across from each other or side to side so many nights over a period of nine months, I think he knows my capabilities and my limitations musically and vocally. And he got into learning chords with me. The chords I wanted to play, but I didn't know what they were, we kinda learned the chords together.

*What was it like playing the Viper Room? That must have been a different experience.*

It was kinda like playing a bloody honky-tonk in the Fifties. That kind of attitude, like "Let's have fun." And it's a very small place, smaller, actually, than the early years. If I feel like I can just go onstage with my guitar and sing my songs, I can't do wrong no matter where I am.

*When you played Fez, in New York, it was quite the scene. The place was crawling with models. Did you notice that?*

Well, of course I noticed that! There were lots of models.

*You're a red-blooded man, after all.*

Yeah. I did notice that. Kate Moss was there. I didn't know the others' names, really.

*How did you hook up with Kate Moss for your "Delia's Gone" video?*

I like the way you put that, "hook up with." [*Laughs*] She was in the video before I was. They said, "Kate Moss is doing it for you," and I said, "Fine, great."

*Were you surprised when U2 came calling last year to have you do "The Wanderer" on "Zooropa"?*

Nope. We've been friends with those guys about seven or eight years. They've been to my home in Tennessee twice. Bono had been to my show before, when I played Dublin, but this time three of 'em came: the Edge and Larry Mullen and Bono. And I got them out onstage with me at the end of the show to sing "Big River." That was really quite a party. Bono wrote down his verse in the palm of his hand. He was singin' looking at his hand. 'Course, he had that perpetual cigarette in his other hand. After the show, he asked me if I would come by the studio the next day and listen to a song he wrote for me. And we put down the track that day. I didn't have any idea it was going to be on the album — he says, "We're just recording some experimental music."

*When you listen to your daughter Rosanne's autobiographical songs about, uh, drinking and wildness and running around, do you admire her songwriting, or do you get a fatherly twinge of "Hey, that's my daughter!"?*

No, I never get that fatherly twinge. Not at all. You know, I've been down that same road she has, it's just something I can relate to and love her more for, because she's overcome it. I wasn't smart enough to do it that young. I admire her very much. And her songwriting, too. She wrote a great song about me called "My Old Man."

*Are you a fan of modern country music?*

I've always been a fan of a little of it. I'm a traditionalist. I like the old traditional country music. I like George Jones, Jimmie Rodgers, the Carter Family, early Gene Autry, Hank Snow. That, to me, was the seminal country music, and to me, it's still the best. Whereas country now has gotten to, I think, the age now of electronic, push-button, TV, video and all that, and special effects. I don't listen to a lot of country music, no. I don't listen to a lot of rock, either. I listen to a little of both. I listen to everything once.

*Last question. I heard that just before you return rental cars, you stuff Big Macs under the seat as a prank.*

That's a new one. I haven't heard that one. I never have done that. You don't know about the other things, but that's

OK. I haven't done that, but maybe it's because I didn't think of it.

*OK, well, thank you for . . .*

Listen, before you go, I want to tell you something I haven't told anybody else.

*Please.*

You know my album cover with the two dogs on it? I've given them names. Their names are Sin and Redemption. Sin is the black one with the white stripe; Redemption is the white one with the black stripe. That's kind of the theme of that album, and I think it says it for me, too. When I was really bad, I was not all bad. When I was really trying to be good, I could never be all good. There would be that black streak going through.

OPPOSITE: CASH *in 1994.* TOP: *June, Johnny Depp, Kate Moss, and Johnny Cash in 1994. Moss appeared in the video for "Delia's Gone."* BOTTOM: *The cover of "American Recordings," 1994.*

# JOHNNY CASH

# WON'T

# BACK DOWN

### By
### ANTHONY DeCURTIS

**O**N A SUNLIT AFTERNOON, Johnny Cash sits in a large, comfortable chair in the Hendersonville, Tennessee, house he's shared with his wife, June Carter Cash, for more than thirty years. He's reflecting on his life. In 1997 he announced that he was struggling with a nervous-system disorder, and his public manifestations since then have been rare. But this afternoon, he is expansive, good-humored and, above all, indomitable as he talks about the album he is

RS 852 • OCTOBER 26, 2000

recording, his plans and his past. "This room right here that you're in, this is the room I moved into when I decided to quit drugs in 1968," Cash says as he looks around the oval-shaped, dark-wooded den. "They didn't have treatment centers the way they do now, so this is the room that I climbed the walls in for thirty days.

"The doctor came to see me every day at 5 P.M.," he continues. "The first few days I was still rollin' stones. Amphetamine was my drug of choice, and I had pills hidden all over this room." He looks over to the many doors that line the wall opposite the row of windows overlooking Old Hickory Lake. He pauses, then laughs to himself. "I was serious about quitting but not quite," he says, wryly. "About the third or fourth day, the doctor looked me in the eye and asked, 'How you doin'?' I said, 'Great!' And he said, 'Bullshit. I know you're not doing great. When are you going to get rid of them?' So I went and got them out of the closet and wherever else I had them hid, and we flushed them. Then I really started the program that he laid out for me. I came out of here feeling like a million dollars."

Being around Johnny Cash is a daunting experience. He is tall, and, though the illness he now lives with has broadened him around the middle and grayed that sleek mane of black hair, he remains a formidable physical presence. As he talks, he will occasionally put his hands over his eyes and rub them, as if he is in pain. Those eyes look as though they have seen everything, have absorbed all the lessons those experiences had to offer and now are hungry for more. His intelligence is keen, and his innate dignity informs every move he makes and every word he speaks. It is heartbreaking to watch him, a giant, struggle with his burden. The knowledge that Cash has walked both sides of the line separating sin and salvation only thickens the air of integrity that always surrounds him.

Right now, in the bright sunshine outside, a celebration is under way on the sprawling grounds of the Cash estate, just north of Nashville. Several hundred people — including such Nashville luminaries as George Jones, Tom T. Hall and Skeeter Davis — have gathered to celebrate the release of June Carter Cash's *Press On*, a moving collection of songs that honors her heritage as a daughter of the Carter Family, the founding family of country music. But while the festivities go on, guests are quietly led back to the house for private audiences with Johnny.

He's friendly to everyone, but he's pacing himself. He plans to perform a song with June in an hour or two, and he needs to conserve his energy.

In October 1997 Cash grew dizzy and nearly fell after bending down to retrieve a guitar pick during a performance in Flint, Michigan. He then told the audience that he had Parkinson's disease. Shortly afterward, he was diagnosed with Shy-Drager syndrome, a progressive, Parkinson's-like illness for which there is currently no cure. [Later, Cash learned that he didn't suffer from Shy-Drager either. Rather, he had autonomic neuropathy, a disorder of the nervous system.] He has subsequently been hospitalized a number of times for pneumonia. Yet Cash has fought his illness with characteristic will — so much so that there is now some question about whether the diagnosis of Shy-Drager is correct. While he suffers many bad days — and neither his doctors nor anyone in the Cash camp will publicly venture a more optimistic read on his health — Cash has fared far better than anyone had a right to believe he would.

It's hardly surprising, under such circumstances, that Cash's mind would turn to an earlier physical struggle — his tormented battle with drug addiction, a battle that, despite some notable backsliding, he eventually won. He does not like discussing his sickness. "It's all right," he assured the Michigan crowd after revealing his illness. "I refuse to give it some ground in my life." In the spring of 1999, he told *USA Today*, "I've made it a point to forget the name of the disease and not to give it any space in my life, because I just can't do it. I can't think that negatively. I can't believe I'm going to be incapacitated. I won't believe that." After that article appeared, Cash was so upset about its detailed discussion of his illness that he canceled some upcoming interviews.

Back in Hendersonville, Cash eventually leaves the house and, dressed in black tails and a black shirt, greets the family members, friends and guests who, to a person, are thrilled to see him. He takes the stage set up in the yard and affectionately introduces June. He looks flushed, and he moves with great deliberateness, spending his store of energy carefully, anticipating the exhaustion to come. Johnny joins June and her band — which includes their son, John Carter Cash, on acoustic guitar — to perform on "The Far Side Banks of Jordan," a tune that Cash first played for

his wife twenty-five years before, telling her, "This is going to be our song." It's the sort of folk spiritual he used to sing with his family on their front porch in Dyess, Arkansas, decades ago, the kind of song that first sparked his love for music. He begins the song, accompanying himself on acoustic guitar. "I believe my steps are growing wearier each day," he sings. "Got another journey on my mind/The lures of this old world/Have ceased to make me want to stay/And my one regret is leaving you behind."

Johnny and June harmonize on the chorus: "I'll be waiting on the far side banks of Jordan/I'll be sitting, drawing pictures in the sand/And when I see you coming/I will rise up with a shout/And come running through the shallow water/Reaching for your hand."

❦ ❦ ❦ ❦ ❦ ❦

**D**ESPITE, OR PERHAPS because of his illness, interest in Johnny Cash's music has reached a fever pitch. In May, Columbia/American/Legacy released an extraordinary three-CD box set of his work. Titled *Love, God, Murder,* it is a thematically organized collection that explores the three grand subjects of Cash's

CASH WITH FAMILY (*John Carter Cash, left*) *and friends (Billy Bob Thornton, second from right) at the Carter homestead in Virginia to celebrate June's birthday in June 2001*

forty-six-year career. Cash has also just released a stunning new album, *American III: Solitary Man,* his third collaboration with producer Rick Rubin. It is an unflinching confrontation with his own mortality, the nearly inconceivable notion of leaving behind all the joys and sorrows that constitute a life. It's hard to imagine anyone else making an album remotely like it.

Like so many of the titanic heroes of rock & roll, Johnny Cash is a glorious mess of contradictions. The wild drugs and debauchery of Saturday night – and, in Cash's case, pretty much every other night, too – have fought vigorously for his soul against the powerful Christian conviction of Sunday morning. Cash is the Man in Black, the noble outlaw, a fearsome figure whose Mount Rushmore face, dark eyes and uproarious excesses helped make him one of the more combustible ingredients in the critical mass that exploded in Memphis in the mid-Fifties. In early songs like "I Walk the Line" and "Big River," he articulated a fierce vi-

sion of what country music – and its bastard child, rock & roll – could be. He hammered out a sound that was bare to the bone, without a single wasted note.

❊ ❊ ❊ ❊ ❊ ❊

WAS A JOHNNY CASH FREAK," says Keith Richards, who first heard Cash's music as a teenager in England. "Luther Perkins, his guitar player, was amazing. Johnny's singing was, too. They taught me about the importance of silence in music – that you don't have to play all over the song. You just play what's necessary. If it's done wrong, it can be painfully monotonous. But when it's done right, it has this incredibly powerful focus and intensity, and that's what those early Cash songs were like.

"As far as early rock & roll goes," Richards continues, "if someone came up to me and for some reason they could only get a collection of one person's music, I'd say, 'Chuck Berry is important, but, man, you've got to get the Cash!' "

While he was making that groundbreaking music, Cash was also inventing what would soon become the myth of Johnny Cash. It is a larger-than-life persona that has had at least as much impact and influence as the music itself. "I was backstage at the Grand Ole Opry in Nashville when I met him in 1965," says Kris Kristofferson, whose career Cash helped to launch. "It was back in his dangerous days, and it was electric. He was skinny as a snake, and you just never knew what he was going to do. He looked like he might explode at any minute. He was a bad boy, he stood up for the underdog, he was exciting and unpredictable, and he had an energy onstage that was unlike anybody else.

_JOHNNY AND JUNE,_
_with John Carter Cash,_
_1994. "My parents had_
_a great forgiveness,_
_and a great accept-_
_ance," says John._

"I shook hands with him," Kristofferson continues, "and that was probably what brought me back to Nashville to be a songwriter. He was everything I thought an artist ought to be."

Folk singer Eric Andersen remembers being introduced to Cash by Bob Dylan at the Newport Folk Festival in 1964. Dylan greatly admired Cash, and Cash, breaking ranks with Nashville orthodoxy, was an early, enthusiastic supporter of Dylan. "I was backstage, and Bob ran over and grabbed me," Andersen recalls. " 'You've gotta meet Johnny Cash, man!' Cash was a hero to us, one of the original cats. So Bob brought me back to his tent, and I met John. He had just done his set, and he was really wired. He looked like a puppet whose strings were all tangled up – half cut, and half held together – and he was just jiggling around."

That darker, uncontrolled side of Cash has drawn generations of fans to him even as many of his contemporaries and their progeny have fallen out of favor. He is, after all, the man who, in "Folsom Prison Blues," sang "I shot a man in Reno/Just to watch him die" in 1955, decades before gangsta rap was born. He demolished hotel rooms and stomped out the lights on the stage of the Grand Ole Opry while Keith Moon was still in short pants.

Those experiences also make Cash, who is now sixty-eight, sympathetic when younger musicians are attacked for causing violence by singing and rapping about it in their songs. "I don't think music and movies have anything to do with it," Cash says, when asked about the relationship between violence and popular culture. "I think it's in the person. I mean, I'm an entertainer. 'I shot a man in Reno/Just to watch him die' is a fantasy. I didn't shoot anybody in Reno – and I didn't kill Delia," he adds with a chuckle, referring to a grisly folk song he adapted on his 1994 _American Recordings_ album.

"But it's fun to sing about those things," he continues. "Murder ballads go way back in country music. Even the Carter Family, they got some really bloody records. There's 'The Banks of the Ohio,' with all that 'stuck a knife in her breast and watched her as she went down under the water, and the bubbles came up out of her mouth, and the water turned red.' And Jimmie Rodgers – 'I'm gonna buy me a shotgun/Just as long as I'm tall/And I'm gonna shoot poor Thelma/Just to see her jump and fall.' That's right up there with 'shot a man in Reno.'

"But these songs are just for singing, and singers always knew that. I'm not suggesting that anybody consider learning how to shoot a gun. I'm not suggesting that they even own one. Although I do. I used to collect antique Colt pistols. But they weren't for shooting. They were like ancient coins. I collect those, too. But the coins aren't for spending, and the guns aren't for shooting."

Inevitably, the discussion about violence leads to the deeply held religious beliefs that are the other pull in Cash's divided soul. They are the salve to the urges most aptly described in the title of a Nick Lowe song he covered a few years back: "The Beast in Me." "There's something missing there," Cash says. "There's a spiritual hunger in people for goodness and righteousness. There's an emptiness in people that they're trying to fill. And I don't know why they go about it the way they do."

Bono recalls visiting Cash in Hendersonville during a drive across the U.S. He and U2 bassist Adam Clayton sat down for a meal with Johnny and June. "We bowed our heads and John spoke this beautiful, poetic grace," Bono says, "and we were all humbled and moved. Then he looked up afterward and said, 'Sure miss the drugs, though.' "

Cash is content to let his convictions, however conflicted, speak for themselves. "I believe what I say, but that don't necessarily make me right," he says, laughing. "There's nothing hypocritical about it. There is a spiritual side to me that goes real deep, but I confess right up front that I'm the biggest sinner of them all." He even views his battle with drug addiction in spiritual terms. "I used drugs to escape," he says quietly, "and they worked pretty well when I was younger. But they devastated me physically and emotionally — and spiritually. That last one hurt so much: to put myself in such a low state that I couldn't communicate with God. There's no lonelier place to be. I was separated from God, and I wasn't even trying to call on him. I knew that there was no line of communication. But he came back. And I came back."

That sense of spiritual wisdom garnered through grueling experience has given Cash the moral strength, as an artist and a person, to always stand his ground. Throughout his life Cash has pandered to no specific audience or constituency. In the Sixties and early Seventies, he performed for American troops and protested the Vietnam War. He defended Native American rights long before it became fashionable. He has both played in prisons and supported organizations that assist the families of slain police officers. And he stands by his friends.

"I opened for John in Philadelphia a few years ago, and I dedicated a song to Mumia Abu-Jamal," Kristofferson recalls. Abu-Jamal is an African-American journalist who is currently on death row for allegedly murdering a police officer — in Philadelphia. His case has become a flash point for activists, who believe Abu-Jamal was railroaded and who want him to get a new trial. It's a flash point as well for law enforcement organizations, which view him as a cold-blooded killer. "The police at the show went ballistic,"

Kristofferson continues. "After I came off, they said that I had to go out and make an apology. I felt pretty bad, because it was John's show. But John heard about it and said to me, 'Listen, you don't need to apologize for nothin'. I want you to come out at the end of the show and do "Why Me" with me.' So I went out and sang with him. John just refuses to compromise."

✿ ✿ ✿ ✾ ✾ ✾

JOHNNY CASH BECAME a superstar in his midtwenties, enjoying an impressive run of hits between 1956 and 1958 on Sun Records. Like Elvis Presley, Cash soon left Sun to sign with a major label, in his case, Columbia. On Columbia, his success continued, beginning with "All Over Again" and the classic "Don't Take Your Guns to Town" in 1958. "Ring of Fire" (1963) was his next major hit, and it's a song with a gripping story behind it.

Cash first laid eyes on June Carter when, on a high school class trip, he saw her perform with the Carter Family at the Grand Ole Opry. When he met her in person backstage at the Opry six years later, he told her, "You and I are going to get married someday." June laughed and said she couldn't wait. The only problem was, she already was married. Of course, Cash was married himself, so nothing much happened until 1962, when June joined Cash's roadshow. "Ring of Fire," composed by June and country star Merle Kilgore, is the story of those first, overwhelming feelings of danger, lust and love.

"I never talked much about how I fell in love with John," June recalls about writing the song. "And I certainly didn't tell him how I felt. It was not a convenient time for me to fall in love with him — and it wasn't a convenient time for him to fall in love with me. One morning, about four o'clock, I was driving my car just about as fast as I could. I thought, 'Why am I out on the highway this time of night?' I was miserable, and it all came to me: 'I'm falling in love with somebody I have no right to fall in love with.'

"I was frightened of his way of life," she continues. "I'd watched Hank Williams die. I was part of his life — I'm Hank Jr.'s godmother — and I'd grieved. So I thought, 'I can't fall in love with this man, but it's just like a ring of fire.' I wanted so to play the song for John, but I knew he would see right through me. So I gave it to my sister Anita, and she recorded it — her version was like a folk song, like bells ringing in the mountains. When John heard it, he said, 'I want to do that song.'"

Cash, needless to say, knew exactly what the song was about from the start. "I remember she had some lyrics," Cash says. "She had a line where she called herself 'the fire-ring woman,' and then she changed that. I said, 'You got it right when you called yourself a "fire-ring woman," because that's exactly where I am.' We hadn't really pledged our love – we hadn't said, 'I love you.' We were both afraid to say it, because we knew what was going to happen: that eventually we were both going to be divorced, and we were going to go through hell. Which we did.

"But the 'ring of fire' was not the hell," he continues. "That was kind of a sweet fire. The ring of fire that I found myself in with June was the fire of redemption. It cleansed. It made me believe everything was all right, because it felt so good. When we fell in love, she took it upon herself to be responsible for me staying alive. I didn't think I was killing myself, but you're on the suicide track when you're doing what I was doing. Amphetamines and alcohol will make you crazy, boy!

"She'd take my drugs and throw them away, and we'd have a big fight over it. I'd get some more, and she'd do it again. I'd make her promise not to, but she would do it anyway." He laughs, "She'd lie to me. She'd hide my money. She'd do anything. She fought me with everything she had."

By the time June and Johnny got married in 1968, his career had reached another peak. The live album he released that year, *At Folsom Prison*, sold extremely well. Then, in 1969, he enjoyed the biggest hit of his career, albeit with a novelty song, Shel Silverstein's "A Boy Named Sue." He began hosting his own network television series, *The Johnny Cash Show*, and used it as a forum for a bold array of musical talent, from Bob Dylan (who appeared on the opening show) to Louis Armstrong, Pete Seeger, Linda Ronstadt and Carl Perkins.

As the Seventies progressed, however, Cash's star waned. Early in the decade, the singer-songwriter movement in rock and the outlaw movement in country provided him with aesthetic vindication and a raft of spiritual heirs. But he shared nothing with later phenomena like disco and the urban cowboy craze, and the connections between his music and punk rock would only become apparent later. The glitz-obsessed Eighties and the onslaught of MTV did little to help matters. Cash made some strong albums in

this period – and some bad ones – but he seemed to have lost his artistic compass.

He remained a powerful draw on the road, however, and in 1985 he joined the Highwaymen, an occasional alliance with Willie Nelson, Waylon Jennings and Kris Kristofferson that would continue until the onset of his illness. In the meantime, Rosanne Cash, a daughter from his first marriage, and June's daughter Carlene both launched their own musical careers. For her part, Rosanne remembers her struggle to escape her father's looming shadow. "I was very rebellious," she says. "I couldn't stand the constant references to him. I wanted to do it on my own. That's not unlike any person in their early twenties, but it just so happened that my dad was very public, so I had to rebel a little harder – and I rose to that test [*laughs*]." That her father was experiencing his own career woes only exacerbated the situation. "When I was having hit records, my dad and I felt competitive with each other," Rosanne says. "He admitted it later. I mean, he would ask me about my contract and how many points I was getting [*laughs*]. We went through that phase. But when he felt that I was pulling away from him, he gave me a lot of space. I think it probably hurt him some."

Cash regained a focus in his work after meeting producer Rick Rubin in the early Nineties. "From the very beginning, I couldn't see what he saw in me," Cash says, bluntly. But Rubin felt he understood exactly who Johnny Cash was. "He's a timeless presence," Rubin says. "From the beginning of rock & roll, there's always been this dark figure who never really fit. He's still the quintessential outsider. In the hip-hop world you see all these bad-boy artists who are juggling being on MTV and running from the law. John was the originator of that."

The three albums Cash and Rubin have made together, *American Recordings* (1994), *Unchained* (1996) and now *Solitary Man*, have helped Cash discover a voice suitable both to a man of his age, disposition and accomplishments and to contemporary times. *American Recordings* received a Grammy for Best Contemporary Folk Album, while *Unchained* won for Best Country Album.

"From the first day, working with Rick has been easy, laid-back, relaxed and trustworthy," Cash says. "We trusted each other to be honest. I said, 'I'm gonna sing you a song and if you don't like it, you tell me. And if you got a song that you like and I don't, you've got to listen to me. I can't sing it if I don't like it.' But he's come up with some really fine songs, and he never pushed anything on me. We get along beautifully."

*Solitary Man* typically reflects the wide range of music that has shaped Johnny Cash's soul. "There's a Bert Williams song written in about 1905 called 'Nobody,'" Cash recounts. "You ever hear 'Nobody'? [*Starts to sing*] I ain't never done nothin' to nobody/I ain't ever got nothin' from nobody no time/And until I get something from somebody sometime/I don't intend to do nothin' for nobody no time." He laughs, clears his throat and begins again: "When wintertime comes with its snow and sleet/ And me with hunger and cold feet/Who says, 'Here's two bits, go and eat'?/Nobody."

He laughs again. "It's a great old song," he says. "Then there's a new song I'm recording next session called 'The Mercy Seat' – it's a Nick Cave song. And I'm writing three or four songs myself at the same time. It's the first time I've ever had them bombard my brain like that. I hadn't written for

FAMILY AFFAIR: WITH *his eldest daughter, Rosanne Cash, in 2001*

more than a year since I got sick, but when I started recording, the ideas started coming. I'll finish them as we work."

For his part, Rubin also found some songs for Cash, including Neil Diamond's "Solitary Man," which became the title track, and Tom Petty's "I Won't Back Down," the album's opening song. Cash was unable to put in long days in the studio, but, according to Rubin, his illness didn't really affect their work together. "He's been fine; we just have to take breaks," he explains. "Whenever he feels comfortable, we record. It's been very pleasant."

The process of working on the album energized Cash. Even the setting proved restorative. "We're recording in a log cabin in the woods, right straight across the road from my house," Cash says. "I built it in '78, and it's just one room. It's got a kitchen, a bathroom off the back and state-of-the-art equipment. We're surrounded by goats, deer, peacocks and crows. We have to stop taping sometimes because the goats get on the porch and tromp around."

Rubin was similarly inspired by the locale. "It feels appropriate, him singing these songs in that environment," he says of the studio. "Lyrically, this album is intense, but musically it's relaxed.

"One thing is a little bit different," Rubin adds a moment later, thinking back to the question of Cash's health and its

impact on their work. "John is a little more self-conscious about his vocals. There's no need for him to be – they're spectacular. But when he listens to them, he often feels, 'I can do better than that.' Meanwhile, everyone in the room is like, 'That was amazing.' I think because he doesn't feel well physically all the time, he's projecting that onto the work. But I don't hear it. I hear these strong, beautiful songs.

"He loves music – it is his life," Rubin says. "After one session, he said to me, 'You know, I think this is going to be my best album ever.' He's made, what, 200 albums? It's exciting to be around someone who's done that much work and still wants to make his best album."

*Grace* is a word that suggests both spiritual blessings and dignity of action, and both of those definitions fully apply to *Solitary Man*. He turns in a splendid version of U2's "One." His voice does falter a bit on "I Won't Back Down," but while the song seemed in search of a meaning when Tom Petty sang it (and Petty turns up on this version as well), in Cash's hands it takes on a staggering gravity. That refusal to go gently gets picked up in Will Oldham's scarifying "I See a Darkness," on which Cash sings, "You know I have a drive to live/I won't let go/But can you see/Its opposition comes rising up sometimes. . . . And that I see a darkness?"

Cash plans to start working on a new album right away. As Rick Rubin said, music is Cash's life. "I didn't like that 'public figure' business," Cash says. "I didn't like that 'American statesman' stuff. I didn't like that 'great spiritual leader' stuff. I am a very private person about those things. So many times, when there would be something I'd have to do that I didn't have my heart in, I'd say, 'All I ever wanted to do was play my guitar and sing a simple song.' And that's still all I want to do."

HESE DAYS, Johnny Cash doesn't have to do anything he doesn't want to do. In a merciless way, illness can clarify your life. "Yeah, well, most of 'em are dead," he says with a grim insouciance when asked if he ever sees any of the people with whom he helped create rock & roll. "Carl Perkins and his brothers are all dead. Bill Black. Elvis. Roy Orbison, who was not only my best friend but my next-door neighbor for twenty years.

"Of the ones who are still left, I talk to Marshall Grant, who played bass for me for so long. He and I are friends. [Producer] Jack Clement and I are still really close. We don't really do a lot of 'good ol' days' sessions, but if something comes up, we'll argue about who's right about it. But I don't see many of them, no. I don't see many people at all since I got sick."

The Carter Family's staunch Appalachian will to survive courses in June's blood, along with a Southern woman's determination to cheerfully make the best out of whatever travails fate may bring. She is now seventy-one, and her devotion to her husband is absolute. "Even now, since John's been sick, we've just had so much fun," she says. "When he first got ill, I said, 'We're going to quit work for a year, and then we'll see how we feel.' And we'll quit another year if we want to. Who says we have to work? We've got a lot of front porches – we'll go sit on them."

"There's unconditional love there," says Cash about his marriage. "You hear that phrase a lot, but it's real with me and her. She loves me in spite of everything, in spite of myself. She has saved my life more than once. She's always been there with her love, and it has certainly made me forget the pain for a long time, many times. When it gets dark, and everybody's gone home and the lights are turned off, it's just me and her."

Johnny and June spend as much time as they can with their family, and they travel among their homes in Tennessee, Virginia and Jamaica. Despite being a longtime road horse, Cash will not be able to tour in support of *Solitary Man*. "It depresses him," says Rosanne. "He's not used to sitting around. He's a very powerful person, and to not feel well, that's really hard for him. He spent over forty years on the road, and suddenly he's not out there. When that energy comes to a screeching halt, there's a lot to deal with just inside yourself."

Whatever he needs to deal with, either inside or outside himself, Johnny Cash will make do and not complain. He doesn't know any other way. "I wouldn't trade my future for anyone's I know," he writes in the liner notes to *Solitary Man*. "I believe that everything I've done and lived through is what has brought me to this part of my life right now," he says, as he looks around his den and remembers the many roads, rough and smooth, he's traveled down. "I like to say I have no regrets. And I really don't."

*"I DIDN'T LIKE THAT 'public figure' business," said Cash. "All I ever wanted to do was play my guitar and sing a simple song."*

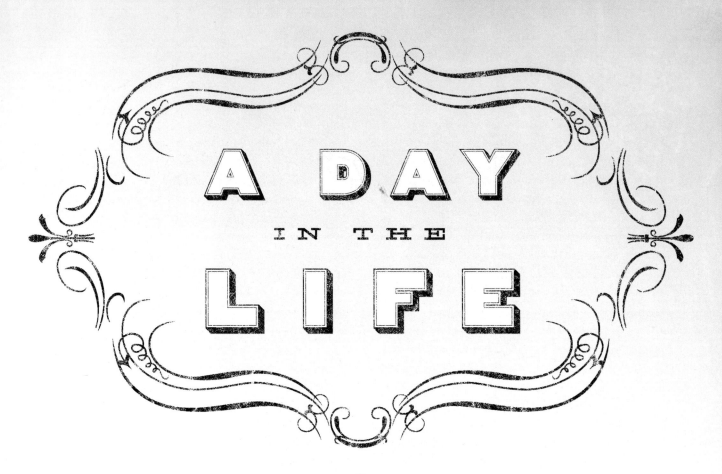

# A DAY IN THE LIFE

### By
### JASON FINE

**M**OST DAYS, Johnny Cash is up by 4 A.M. He goes downstairs, brews coffee and turns on the news. He might fall back to sleep for an hour or so in his black leather recliner, then he shaves, showers and puts on some clothes. His next few hours will be spent in a grand living room overlooking Old Hickory Lake, north of Nashville, listening to the Thirties and Forties

AT HOME IN HENDER-
sonville, October 2002.
"To tell you the truth, I
don't think about death
at all," Cash said.
"What's to think about?
I enjoy my life now."

**RS 911 • DECEMBER 12, 2002**

gospel groups that he loves more than anything else right now.

By then it's 9 A.M. That's when the trouble starts. "I'll sit there with June and I say, 'June, what do I do now? What in the world do I do now?' And she says, 'John, you don't have to do anything, just rest.' And I say, 'I'm not tired. And I'm not sick. I got to do something with this day.' "

Sometimes they go shopping. "I go to Dillard's or Wal-Mart with June and just hang out with her," says Cash, who's been married to June Carter Cash since 1968. "So long as she's shopping, so long as she's moving, I follow. I'm a great shopper. I buy shirts and records. I've got too many shirts already, most of them black."

Johnny Cash turned seventy in February, and the years wear hard. At first, it's jarring to see him – heavy, unsteady on his feet, that famous shock of black hair gone white.

Cash has diabetes, and he's been in and out of the hospital with pneumonia – serious enough to put him in a coma for eight days in October 2001. Glaucoma has stolen most of his eyesight; asthma keeps him fighting for breath. (In 1999, Cash was misdiagnosed with Shy-Drager syndrome, a Parkinson's-like neurological disorder he says he knew he never had. "An old man knows in his bones if he's got a debilitating disease," he says. "And I knew I didn't have that one.")

Even as he struggles for breath, Cash radiates a fierce determination. For forty-seven years, he has made music that fuses two dark traditions: rustic religious fatalism and reckless self-abandon. He has recorded with Elvis Presley, Bob Dylan and Bono, as well as Fiona Apple, Nick Cave and Sheryl Crow. His legend surrounds him, and you can't help being convinced when he says age and illness don't scare him – he's faced down death so many times before. "To tell you the truth, I don't think about death at all," Cash says. "What's to think about? I enjoy my life now." He talks openly, and with humor, about his years of drug abuse and illness, and he admits that even now the old demons lurk. "They don't come knocking on a regular basis," he says. "They just kind of hold their distance. I could invite them in: the sex demon, the drug demon. But I don't. They're very sinister. You got to watch 'em." He laughs. "They'll sneak up on you. All of a sudden there'll be a beautiful little Percodan laying there, and you'll want it."

Cash quit touring in 1997, after forty-two years on the road, but he continues to make music at a remarkable pace. His new album, *American IV: The Man Comes Around*, is the fourth in a sterling run with producer Rick Rubin. The song choice is ballsy – from a version of Nine Inch Nails' "Hurt" that Cash makes even more isolated and painful than the original to a hymnlike interpretation of Simon and Garfunkel's "Bridge Over Troubled Water." Cash's voice is shaky in places, but the cracks and slurs add to its ragged grandeur. "At one point, I said to Rick, 'We're really getting sad and mournful with this album,' " Cash says. "And he said, 'Not depression-sad, just sad for the sake of sadness.' After that, I thought, you know, if that's what's coming, let's go for it." They did. Especially on Cash's version of the traditional "Danny Boy," there is the feeling of a final message being delivered.

Now, Cash has begun work on a new album of gospel songs, including favorites by the Golden Gate Quartet and the Five Blind Boys of Alabama: "I've always wanted to do black gospel, and I know I'm a little tight-ass saying 'black' – I'm a honky – but I feel like I need to do it. I feel like it's going to be all right." After that, he wants to do an album called *Grass Roots* – a survey of folk and country songs "all the way back to Stephen Foster." Asked if he might retire, he snaps, "No, no, no, no, no. I'd die if I retire. Like a shark – got to keep moving."

The Cash home is a majestic wood-and-glass modern castle set into the limestone cliffs above Old Hickory Lake. Some of the log beams were salvaged from pioneer barns along the nearby Cumberland River. Ornate chandeliers, dark rugs and antique wooden furniture fill the rooms. Cash's office is the smallest room in the house – not much bigger than a tour bus bunk. A window looks out over his old fishing dock and the glassy gray lake. "This is about my favorite place," he says, sitting at his desk on a cloudy November morning. "I don't need all that space." He wears a denim work shirt with the Sun

Records logo on it, black work pants, black sneakers and blue socks. Around him, the walls are lined with books — volumes on religion, folk music, American literature and politics. Nixon's memoirs sit next to a thick history of the Aztecs; a book of Christian hymns hides behind a box of Winchester bullets. Cash's eyesight is so bad that he can't read anymore. "It's a room of regrets now," he says. "I miss my books."

Cash reaches for a guitar carved from a Virginia mulberry tree. His hands are swollen, but he picks through two traditional gospel tunes easily, and then his own "Half a Mile a Day," which he plans to include on the new album. Cash wrote the song twenty years ago but came back to it now, he says, "because I wasn't satisfied."

This afternoon, Johnny and June Cash plan to go to the studio he's built out of a one-room log cabin on a remote part of his property. They'll record vocals for Cash's album and for a solo album June is making. Cash is itching to get to work, but first he wants breakfast. He's on a no-salt, no-sugar diet and eats lighter than he used to, but he confesses, "Sometimes I'll have a breakfast sandwich, which is two fried eggs with crisp bacon on cinnamon toast. It's good, it really is." He pauses. "You want one?"

Breakfast is a big time at the Cashes'. June, radiant at seventy-three, joins us at a formally set dining table. Sand-

wiches arrive for Johnny and me, and June builds her own breakfast invention: cinnamon toast with cream cheese, crushed raspberries and pear preserves made from fruit grown outside the kitchen window.

The Cashes plan to leave for their winter home in Jamaica in two days, and the house is buzzing with cooks and maids making preparations. There's other family business, too. A Cash family member is in trouble with drugs; an intervention is planned for the next morning. Drug abuse, Cash says wearily, "runs through this family like a turkey through the corn. Man, it's terrible. We're just trying to save him, trying to snatch him up before he goes."

Cash seems worn out after breakfast. He's eager to get away. "Jamaica-itis," he says.

"A week down there, we'll have our energy back," June chips in.

Cash smiles at her. "When we get to Jamaica," he says, "there's no stopping us." He stands, leans against a chair for balance and excuses himself for a nap. On the way out, Cash stops and turns back to June. "We'll go over at two," he says. "You and me got some singing to do."

It was built as a getaway, where Johnny Cash and June Carter Cash snuck away to spend quiet weekends, and where their only child together, John Carter Cash, remembers coming to watch movies with his dad. But the one-room log cabin Johnny built in 1979 across the road from his estate in Hendersonville, Tennessee, became the unlikely launching pad for his 1990s comeback — the place he came to play guitar, write and rehearse songs, and record demos, which sometimes ended up as final versions on his four albums for American Recordings.

**HOME SWEET HOME**

**IN THE STUDIO**
**WITH**
**JOHN CARTER CASH**
*By*
**JASON FINE**

Especially in Johnny's last years, as he grew less mobile, the cabin became the studio he used to record many of the songs for his final two albums, *American III: Solitary Man* (2000), and *American IV: The Man Comes Around* (2002). John, 33, was an associate producer and co-engineer on those albums; he also produced his mother's last two albums, *Press On* and *Wildwood Flower,* partly in the cabin. In the past year, John has added a second room and opened the studio to other artists, but basically it's the same wooden box, with a small mixing console tucked into a corner next to the fireplace, a dusty sofa beneath the blanket-covered window and three weather-beaten chairs out on the porch.

CASH IN HIS LOG CABIN *studio, in 1994 — the same year he released "American Recordings"*

The cabin overlooks fifty acres of scrubby, sloping hills that are home to a dwindling herd of multihued fallow deer and goats. It's the last of Johnny's impressive menagerie, which once included ostriches, peacocks and two buffalos, Rufus and Clementine, who often disrupted recording sessions when they scraped their horns against the cabin's air-conditioning unit. Rufus and Clementine were slaughtered after they gored Johnny's father's pet pig, and John remembers the family eating buffalo meat for a year. He also remembers the night Tom Petty got into a tussle with an emu. "Tom and the boys were back here having a big night," John says. "I remember watching them chase the emus and the ostriches, which," he says with a laugh, "is not a good idea."

On the bright fall morning when I visited, John Carter Cash was finishing work on a Carter Family tribute album that will include his father's last recording. "This is not your conventional studio, that's for sure," he says. "It's more of an 'environmentally rich' recording space. And it's home."

*ABOVE: THE ONE-ROOM cabin Cash built for himself and June became the studio where he relaunched his career.*

*When did your dad start using this space as a studio?*

In '94 we put in a small board and a couple of preamps, a couple of good mikes, and started recording music over here — just my dad and his guitar. If he had had to go to some studio in Nashville to record, I don't think he would have done it. This was his compound in the woods, this was where he could get away and at the same time be right at home.

*He was pretty frail during the recording of "American IV." Did you think it would be his last?*

I stopped thinking a long time ago. Even when he was lying there in the hospital and heading out, I knew he probably wouldn't make it, but I still didn't ever put it past him that he wouldn't get better. Because I'd seen him real down before and he got back up. His spirit was beyond human somehow. He was beyond human in his resilience. He always had that bounce-back thing.

*After your mom died, he went back to recording pretty quickly.*

He went back into the studio ten days after she died, and really started working hard. It's a life lesson that a parent's motto is "Press on." That was the title of my mom's record, *Press On.*

*Yeah, and your dad wrote a song called "Drive On."*

Yeah, "Drive on." There's a lot to say that in the face of pain and misery or struggle, you don't stop.

*Did you and he talk about these things after your mom died?*

We didn't have to talk about it. It's the way that we've lived our lives. He called me on the phone and said, "I gotta get to work, you know." I said, "Oh, man, I do too." That's the deal, that's what keeps us going. And he was always eager. He was ready to go to New York City for the MTV Awards, but he couldn't go because physically, his body stopped him.

*Was he in a lot of pain?*

Yeah, sure. He was in constant pain through the last decade of his life. But he got to a point where he balanced it and he continued to work. What mattered to my dad was that he was persistent. He was the strongest man I've ever known. He never stopped. His heart was always in it. It was a struggle for him to record a lot of the time. But in pain or misery or whether he had to sing a song four or five times or more, it didn't matter. He recorded up until two weeks before he died.

*What was the last thing he recorded?*

The very last thing that he ever recorded was a song called "Engine 143," an old Carter Family traditional. It was him, an acoustic guitar, mandolin and upright bass.

*You were also working on "American V."*

The day before we did "Engine 143," we had a session for *American V* – he recorded a full record. We're beginning to mix it this week here at the cabin. He'd recorded forty-five songs.

*What's the record like?*

It started out as gospel, but he didn't like to have boundaries or restrictions, so if a good song came in he'd always record it. He ended up recording all kinds of stuff, everything from gospel to "Aloha 'Oe." You never knew what he was going to do.

*What's your first memory of music?*

My very first memory of music was when I was very young, two or three years old, being brought out onstage at the end of "A Boy Named Sue." My dad would sing, "and I did have a son, and here he is, John Carter Cash." And he

would introduce me, and I'd come out and take a bow. The first song that I ever performed onstage by myself was called "The Wayworn Traveler," an old Carter Family song. Later, I got more into rock & roll.

*How much time did you spend on the road?*

I went with them pretty much everywhere until I was in first grade. After that, I went with them on the road in the summers, and usually a couple of weeks out of the year if they went overseas. So I traveled a lot, and then after I got out of high school I bounced around a lot in college. But then, at about twenty-four, I went out on the road with them again. I did that until I was twenty-seven, then my dad retired. I'd been on the road for twenty-seven years, so I was ready to stop too. [*Laughs*]

*What did you think when your dad started working with Rick Rubin?*

I thought it was cool. I was working with my dad on the road, so seeing all these younger faces in the crowd was exciting. There were times when I'd

BELOW: FATHER AND son recording "American V" in August 2003, one month before Johnny's death

## The Man Comes Around

*Spoken*

You can be first on the draw
You can kill ~ your mother in Law
You can steal some pilgrims Macinaw
But you gotta know it'll be coming down
When the man comes around —

*V.1*

There's a man going 'round taking names
And decides who to free and who to blame
Everybody won't be treated all the Same
There'll be a golden ladder coming down
When the man comes around

*V.2*

The hairs on your head will stand up
When all you're trying to do is stand up
Will you partake of that last offered cup
Or disappear into the Potters ground
When the man comes around

*1st Chorus*

You will hear ten million trumpets
Ten million angels will be singing
Multitudes are marching
To the big Kettle Drum
Somewhere there are voices crying
Some are borning Some are dying
Alpha and Omega's
On the day of Kingdom Come

---

## Recorded at Cedar Hill Refuge (Cash Cabin Studio) May 17 – 21 1999

1. The Oak and the Willow
2. Mary of the Wild Moor
3. Nobody
4. A Singer of Songs
5. Salty Dog
6. The train don't Stop here Anymore
7. Would you Lay with me
8. I Still Write your name
9. Chattanooga Sugar Babe
10. Field of Diamonds
11. She thinks I Still Care
12. Satisfied Mind
13. Cool Water
14. A Bar with no Beer
15. Hard Times

hear Rick's song suggestions and I'd scratch my head because it wouldn't have been something I'd have picked, but Rick never made a mistake. He had a way.

*Your parents are usually portrayed as the perfect couple. Did they fight like normal parents?*

Oh, my parents went through hard times, they went through struggles. But they had a great forgiveness, and they had a great acceptance. They were closer at the end of my mother's life than they'd ever been before. They had found their peace together. When my mom was gone, a piece of my dad was gone. He missed her; he wanted to be with her.

*What brought your mom back to recording in the last years of her life?*

My dad retired and began to record music in earnest; my mom still had a lot she wanted to say and do too. So it was just a natural course for her to continue to make her own music. Her great statement as an artist, I believe, came with these two records that came out toward the end of her life.

*In one of her songs, "I Used to Be Somebody," she mourns that she'll never get to see old friends like Elvis and James Dean again. She sounds almost unsure if she made the right choices in her life.*

She was a romantic. And she had a great nostalgia about her younger life, but she was also very content in who she became, and what she did with her life. I think everybody looks back and says, "I wonder what would have happened if. . . ." And I think that's the spirit of that song, and also just that tender nostalgia for a period in her life when she was young, excited and at a beginning. But she stayed where she was, and my father also. They didn't go off, they went through their middle age together, and then through their older years together. And there's a great strength there; the older they got, they grew closer together.

*What's the greatest lesson you learned from your mom and dad?*

Tenacity. That stick-to-itiveness. You know, press on. In the face of pain, continue on. And faith in God. A belief in a higher purpose. We all have a direction. We're all capable of being guided if we listen and do the footwork.

*Gotta do the footwork.*

Yeah, that's it, man. Footwork.

TOP: *cash's hand-written lyrics to "The Man Comes Around," 2002.* BOTTOM: *A track listing from a recording session for "American III," 1999.* OPPOSITE: *John, age three, sings "Mary Had a Little Lamb" for his dad's Las Vegas audience, 1973.*

# A CRITICAL DISCOGRAPHY

## By GREG KOT

JOHNNY CASH ONCE SAID, "I'm not much of an entertainer, but I know about a thousand songs." In his forty-eight-year career, Cash recorded all of those and many more, cutting literally thousands of songs and hundreds of albums that make up one of the deepest, most far-ranging catalogs in all of popular music. No matter what he sang—from the oldest folk hymns and spirituals to rock songs by U2 and Soundgarden—Cash had the unique ability to make it all his own. A complete Cash discography could fill several books (indeed, several have been published). Instead, what follows is a guide to Cash's essential work. From his classic Sun singles and career-defining Folsom and San Quentin prison concerts to Sixties concept albums like *Ride This Train* and *Bitter Tears* to long-neglected gems like 1991's *Mystery of Life* to his remarkable last decade with producer Rick Rubin, these are the recordings that define one of the greatest voices in American music.

## THE SUN YEARS
## 1955-58

✳ ✳ ✳ ✳ ✳ ✳

THE ESSENTIALS

"Hey Porter"

*(June 1955)*

"Cry, Cry, Cry"

*(June 1955, No. 14 country)*

"Folsom Prison Blues"

*(December 1955, No. 4 country)*

"So Doggone Lonesome"

*(December 1955, No. 4 country)*

"I Walk the Line"

*(May 1956, No. 1 country, No. 17 pop)*

"Get Rhythm"

*(May 1956, No. 1 country)*

*Johnny Cash*

*With His Hot and Blue Guitar*

*(September 1957)*

"Ballad of a Teenage Queen"

*(December 1957, No. 1 country,*

*No. 14 pop)*

*Johnny Cash Sings: The Songs That*

*Made Him Famous*

*(November 1958)*

*The Essential Sun Singles*

*(April 2002)*

✳ ✳ ✳ ✳ ✳ ✳

WHEN THEY BEGAN RECORDING for Sam Phillips at Sun Studios in Memphis, Johnny Cash and the Tennessee Two were a hillbilly punk band made up of two garage mechanics and a singer with a Grand Canyon-deep voice. Their signature *boom-chicka-boom* chug emerged out of necessity: Luther Perkins played little more than ascending and descending triplets on his guitar, muting the strings with his palm, and Marshall Grant was just learning the upright bass, so Phillips fattened the sound with slap-back echo. Cash's acoustic rhythm guitar was outfitted with paper wound through the strings, which made it sound more like a drum. The stark, rhythm-heavy backdrop suited Cash's baritone. It gave his early singles a gravity and maturity lacking in most of the era's rock & roll, though Cash was barely twenty-three when he cut his first single. At the same time, the records sounded nothing like most country music of that era; without Nashville signifiers such as fiddle and pedal steel, Cash's brand of country sounded rough, earthy, ominous.

Cash's first batch of singles made it apparent that both sonically and lyrically he was on to something new:

PERFORMING *at Massey Hall in Toronto, 1961*

"Cry, Cry, Cry" puts a hard-edged twist on clichéd notions of the country weeper, as Cash oozes contempt for a nightlife-loving girlfriend; in "Folsom Prison Blues," he gets inside the mind of a cold-hearted killer. Then there's the hypnotic pledge of allegiance, "I Walk the Line," a record that still sounds otherworldly, with Cash humming an intro to each verse as it shifts key.

Cash's first album was also Sun's debut long-player: *Johnny Cash With His Hot and Blue Guitar.* It includes his first three singles and additional songs centered on themes he would return to obsessively: trains (Leadbelly's "Rock Island Line" and the traditional "Wreck of the Old '97") and prisons (Hank Williams' "[I Heard That] Lonesome Whistle" and Jimmie Skinner's "Doin' My Time"). The follow-up, *Johnny Cash Sings: The Songs That Made Him Famous,* is a greatest-hits set from his Sun years released after he jumped to Columbia Records. The falsetto-dipped choir tacked onto "Ballad of a Teenage Queen" helped Cash cross over to a teen audience; the song, written and produced by Sun engineer Jack Clement, became Cash's first Number One country hit and his

highest-ranking pop success yet, reaching Number Fourteen. Its B side, "Big River," brings an epic dimension to the singer's recurrent theme of suffering ("I taught the weepin' willow how to cry") and adds a bluesy swagger to his sound, with Clement pecking out the percussive guitar riff.

*The Essential Sun Singles* rounds up twenty-five early performances, including "Give My Love to Rose" (reprised on Cash's last album, *American IV: The Man Comes Around*), in which the singer transforms himself

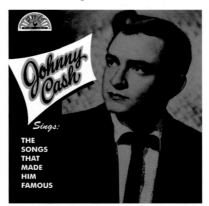

into a dying gunslinger, the first of many songs steeped in Western lore. "Luther Played the Boogie" pays tribute to Cash's not-so-secret weapon, Perkins and his percussive lead guitar. "Play it strange!" Cash exhorts him, and the song becomes a trademark for the "plain ol' hillbilly band" and its revolutionary sound.

* * * * *

FURTHER LISTENING
*Johnny Cash Sings Hank Williams . . .
and Other Favorite Tunes*
(October 1960; June 2003)
*The Man in Black: 1954-1958*
(September 1990)
*The Sun Years*
(January 1990)

*The Million Dollar Quartet
With Elvis Presley, Jerry Lee Lewis and
Carl Perkins (February 1990)
The Complete Original Sun Singles*
(September 1999)
*Roads Less Travelled: The Rare and
Unissued Sun Recordings*
(March 2001)

* * * * *

By 1958, Cash was frustrated by Phillips' reluctance to let him record gospel songs and his below-standard royalty rate at Sun. During that year he recorded mostly cover songs for Phillips, saving his original material for a new deal with Columbia Records. Though he remained Sun's best-selling artist until the label was sold in 1968, most of these later recordings lack the spark of Cash's early singles. They're sullied by the addition of backing choirs, as Phillips tried to compete with more polished pop-country productions from stars like Patsy Cline, Marty Robbins and Buck Owens.

*Sings Hank Williams* and *Roads Less Travelled* show a singer well-acquainted with the vocabulary of high and lonesome. Though the Williams tracks were originally issued with an overdubbed choir, the CD reissue pares the arrangements back to the essentials. *Roads* finds Cash digging deep for a Hank Snow obscurity, a 1920s cowboy ballad and Leon Payne's "I Love You Because," with what sounds like Jerry Lee Lewis (who goes uncredited) honky-tonkin' on piano.

Sun's biggest stars — Lewis, Cash, Elvis Presley and Carl Perkins —

IN THE STUDIO IN 1969, *the same year "At San Quentin" was released*

gathered for an impromptu session at Phillips' studio on December 4th, 1956. But *The Million Dollar Quartet*, essentially an informal jam session, wasn't released until 1990 because it consists mainly of half-finished songs and studio chatter. It also excludes any tracks performed with Cash, even though he appeared in the photos taken at the session and reportedly sang a handful of songs, among them "Blueberry Hill." No recordings from the session with Cash audible on them have ever been found.

## CASH ON COLUMBIA 1958-1960

❋ ❋ ❋ ❋ ❋

THE ESSENTIALS
"All Over Again"
*(September 1958, No. 4 country, No. 38 pop)*
"What Do I Care?"
*(September 1958, No. 7 country)*
*The Fabulous Johnny Cash*
*(November 1958, No. 19 pop)*
"Don't Take Your Guns to Town"
*(December 1958, No. 1 country, No. 32 pop)*
"I Still Miss Someone"
*(December 1958)*
*Hymns by Johnny Cash*
*(May 1959)*
*Songs of Our Soil*
*(September 1959)*

❋ ❋ ❋ ❋ ❋

AFTER COASTING THROUGH HIS final months at Sun, Cash came roaring back with three full-length albums in ten months for Columbia, all of which stand among his finest work. He was given artistic carte blanche by producer Don Law, and *The Fabulous Johnny Cash* was the result. With his Tennessee Two abetted by drummer Buddy Harman and backing vocalists the Jordanaires, Cash broadens his sound to embrace pop, folk and gospel without forsaking his *boom-chicka-boom* sound. He goes honky-tonkin' on "That's All Over," hops the rails on "One More Ride" and embraces the popular folk revival with "Pickin'

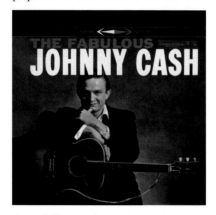

Time." Harman's drumming brings a cinematic drama to the hit "Don't Take Your Guns to Town." The album would go on to sell 400,000 copies.

Next Cash made an album composed exclusively of gospel songs. Neither preachy nor sentimental, *Hymns by Johnny Cash* is sparse and direct, with the Tennessee Two and Harman augmented by touches of piano and pedal steel guitar and a backing choir. The repertoire blends solemn traditionals such as "Swing Low, Sweet Chariot" with Cash originals, notably "It Was Jesus," fired by call-and-response gospel vocals, and "I Call Him," co-written with Cash's older brother Roy.

*Songs of Our Soil*, most of which was recorded in a single March 1959 session, is as good a place as any to look for the roots of Americana, the musical umbrella for alternative country and new folk. It's an album organized around the themes of rural life, home and family, and the cruel cycle of nature. It's anchored by the autobiographical "Five Feet High and Rising," about a Mississippi River flood that nearly consumed the Cash family's Arkansas homestead in the 1930s, and the protest ballad "Old Apache Squaw," in which the singer explicitly acknowledges his empathy for Native Americans.

❋ ❋ ❋ ❋ ❋

FURTHER LISTENING
*Now, There Was a Song!*
*(December 1960)*
*The Man in Black 1959-1962*
*(September 1991)*
*Live at Town Hall Party 1958*
*(May 2003)*
*Live at Town Hall Party 1959*
*(May 2003)*
*Live Recordings From the Louisiana Hayride*
*(September 2003)*

❋ ❋ ❋ ❋ ❋

The *Town Hall* and *Louisiana Hayride* concert recordings document Cash's rapid evolution from Sun Records upstart to Hollywood-endorsed country star. The *Town Hall* shows were both recorded in Compton, California, soon after Cash had moved to Los Angeles. The 1958 appearance catches him breaking in gospel songs and testing new material such as "Don't Take Your Guns to Town." The 1959 concert ups the ante; it's a sexually charged performance before an audience of screaming female fans. A newfound aggression spills over into the prison rant "I Got Stripes," in which the tempo manically accelerates as the song's narrator struggles to bust loose from his chains. Cash's recordings for the

Louisiana Hayride radio program span 1955 to 1963 and include a raucous take on "The Rebel – Johnny Yuma," the theme from a TV Western series in which Cash appeared.

*Now, There Was a Song!* is a tribute to Cash's favorite singers and songwriters, knocked out in a single recording session. Cash tackles tunes by Hank Williams, George Jones and Ernest Tubb, but only "Transfusion Blues," a reworked version of Roy Hogsed's "Cocaine Blues," is a surprise – a veiled attempt, perhaps, at addressing Cash's encroaching difficulties with substance abuse.

## CONCEPT ALBUMS
## 1960-77

✳ ✳ ✳ ✳ ✳

THE ESSENTIALS
*Ride This Train*
(September 1960)
*Blood, Sweat and Tears*
(January 1963)
*Bitter Tears:*
*Ballads of the American Indian*
(September 1964, No. 2 country,
No. 47 pop)
*Johnny Cash Sings the Ballads*
*of the True West*
(September 1965)
*America: A 200-Year Salute*

*in Story and Song*
(July 1972, No. 3 country)
*The Rambler*
(July 1977, No. 31 country)

✳ ✳ ✳ ✳ ✳

AT THE PEAK OF HIS NEW POPULAR- ity, Cash broke with mainstream country formulas to make the first in a series of concept albums – what he called "country operas" – that explored the themes that preoccupied him: the American frontier, trains, Native Americans, wanderlust.

*Ride This Train*, the first and one of the best, is not so much about trains as it is about the people and events one might see from the windows of a passenger car rolling back through time. Most of the songs – which are linked by Cash's Will Rogers-like narration over the sound of a chugging steam engine – are sung in the first person, with Cash playing the role of a convict, a lumberjack, a coal miner, a country doctor and, boldest of all, a slave plantation owner. Stark arrangements frame the lyrics, with Cash at his most conversational, a master storyteller on a roll.

*Blood, Sweat and Tears* opens with the sound of a hammer pounding on rock, which sets the tone for an album filled with hard-bitten tales of disenfranchised workingmen. Stringed instruments underpin chain-gang sound effects and movielike dialogue. With "The Legend of John Henry's Hammer," the album picks up where the plantation narrative "Boss Jack," on *Ride This Train*, left off. It's a man vs. machine folk ballad, an eight-and-a-half-minute epic tale of hard labor and dignity in the face of oppressive working conditions and encroaching

modernity. The sparse instrumentation and sound effects frame the singer's magnetic narrative and delivery, which shifts between a first- and third-person point of view. Cash also lionizes the doomed train engineer Casey Jones and an execution-bound convict in "Another Man Done Gone," a chilling a cappella duet with the Carter Family's Anita Carter: "They hung him in a tree/They let his children see." Even Cash's interpretation of Harlan Howard's "Busted" is somber; it later became a hit in Ray Charles' jocular R&B version.

That air of fatalism turns to anger on *Bitter Tears*, which presaged a rising tide of American Indian activism and a growing sense of outrage about the country's treatment of Native Americans. Cash was deeply moved by the songs of Peter LaFarge, an American Indian folk singer he met while checking out the Greenwich Village folk scene in the early Sixties, and covers five of his songs on *Bitter Tears*. Cash's own songs consistently identified with the oppressed, and he homed in on LaFarge's sense of betrayal to a remarkable extreme. Cash even recorded the songwriter's notorious "Custer," in which the tale of one of the most infamous defeats in American history is

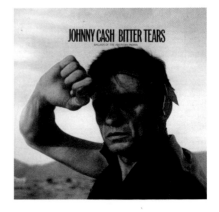

told from a gloating Indian's perspective ("And the general, he don't ride well anymore"). Tribal drumming and solemn chanting showcase Cash's flair for the dramatic, while string-band virtuosos Bob Johnson and Norman Blake ground the album in the folk tradition. "The Ballad of Ira Hayes," a eulogy to the American Indian war hero who died an impoverished alcoholic, overcame initial resistance by country radio to become one of Cash's biggest hits, rising to Number Three on the country chart. In "As Long as the Grass Shall Grow," Cash indicts American presidents for betraying the country's first residents; "White Girl" addresses interracial relationships. As risky as the album was commercially, it established Cash as a credible figure in the emerging counterculture and protest movements. In this respect, he transcended the work of many of his peers; it's impossible to imagine any other member of the Million Dollar Quartet tackling such themes in his music.

Cash brought an emotional authenticity to his most ambitious song cycle, the double album *Johnny Cash Sings the Ballads of the True West.* He writes in the liner notes that to prepare for making the record, "I followed trains in my jeep and on foot. I slept under mesquite bushes and in gullies. . . . I learned to throw a Bowie knife and kill a jack rabbit at 40 yards, not for sport but because I was hungry." He also offers his plainspoken interpretation of America's Manifest Destiny and cutthroat frontier justice, beginning with the Indians' first sighting of the colonists' longboats. Along the way, he attempts to demythologize the shootout at the OK

Corral, recounts the assassination of President James Garfield and the life and death of the serial killer John Wesley Hardin, and honors the Confederate soldier in "Johnny Reb." Cash's music is as sprawling as his subject matter, from campfire

hootenannies on stringed instruments to ornate orchestrations with symphony musicians. His blend of narration and singing is at its most theatrical on "Sam Hall" (reprised on *American IV: The Man Comes Around*), where he impersonates a drunken, bile-spewing convict in the moments before his hanging.

*America: A 200-Year Salute in Story and Song* arrived as the Vietnam War was ripping the nation apart. Instead of the moral reckoning of his best Sixties concept works, Cash strikes a soothing and self-consciously sentimental stance, as if getting a jumpstart on the forthcoming bicentennial celebration. He cheerleads a tour of America's past, name-checking heroes such as Paul Revere, Andrew Jackson and Daniel Boone in another of his homespun oral histories. The sole exception is "Big Foot"; its graphic retelling of the massacre at Wounded Knee echoes the Native American narratives of

*Bitter Tears* eight years earlier. Though Carl Perkins and the Tennessee Three rhythm section of Marshall Grant and W.S. Holland accompany Cash, the music owes little to the singer's country past; instead, there's a rural, folk feel to the arrangements, as defined by the guitars of Norman Blake and Red Lane, Charlie McCoy's harmonica, and Chuck Cochran's piano. Ultimately, it's Cash's power as a storyteller and master of spoken-word performance that carries the album, never more so than on his reading of Abraham Lincoln's Gettysburg Address.

*The Rambler* is a more introspective take on the traveling theme, a narrative about emotional and geographical distance. Once more, the backing is sparse, mostly acoustic, with parlor piano and strings, but the dominating feature is an extended dialogue between two drifters driving cross-country that links the songs. It's not as grand as his earlier concept works, but in many ways it's one of his best albums and one of the most underrated, because it arrived in the late Seventies, when Cash was no longer on the pop or country charts. "Hit the Road and Go" is a relatively lean, Sun Records-style throwback, and it kicks off an album composed entirely of Cash tunes. In them, he converses and sings about the endless road, the inscrutability of love and his own conflicted psyche. "There ain't no man that's all good," says Cash's companion, the Fisherman. "No man is all bad either," Cash the Rambler responds, summing up a career that has traveled both sides of the road.

* * * * *

FURTHER LISTENING

*From Sea to Shining Sea*

(March 1967, No. 9 country)

*Come Along and Ride This Train*

(September 1991)

* * * * *

*From Sea to Shining Sea* is another travelogue that falls between the unabashed flag-waving of *America: A 200-Year Salute in Story and Song* and the cutting commentary of *Bitter Tears*. It's notable mainly because it hints at Cash's deteriorating physical and mental state, due to an ongoing struggle with drugs and alcohol. Hoarseness diminishes his voice's power, and the intro to "Shrimpin'

Sailin'" sounds like the wild-eyed ranting of a speed freak.

The Bear Family label's box set *Come Along and Ride This Train* collects all the concept albums, a huge canvas that lays out the contradictions and complexities of Cash's art. In these works, he's both patriot and protest singer, mythmaking historian and myth-debunking critic. Cash released these song cycles at relatively frequent intervals as his fame escalated, finding in them the ideal story-

JOHNNY CASH SINGS *at the Grand Ole Opry, 1971.*

telling vehicle for expressing his beliefs and values in depth. To get the true measure of Cash, every record collection should include at least a handful of his concept albums.

## "RING OF FIRE" TO "JACKSON" 1963-67

* * * * *

THE ESSENTIALS

"Ring of Fire"

*(April 1963, No. 1 country,*

*No. 17 pop)*

*Ring of Fire:*

*The Best of Johnny Cash*

*(July 1963, No. 1 country,*

*No. 26 pop)*

"It Ain't Me, Babe"

*(October 1964, No. 4 country)*

*Orange Blossom Special*

*(March 1965, No. 3 country,*

*No. 49 pop)*

"Jackson"

*(February 1967, No. 2 country)*

*Carryin' On With Johnny Cash*

*and June Carter*

*(September 1967, No. 5 country)*

* * * * *

JUNE CARTER HAD JUST BEGUN TO perform with Johnny Cash when she conceptualized the lyrics for "Ring of Fire," about their blossoming love affair. The song, co-written by Carter and Merle Kilgore, became one of Cash's biggest hits with its mariachi horn flourishes, and Columbia hastily assembled an album of recent tracks around it, a mix of gospel ("Were You There [When They Crucified My Lord]"), Sun Records-style rockabilly ("Tennessee Flat Top Box"), even the TV theme for *Bonanza*, with lyrics added.

By the mid-Sixties, Cash was spending more time with young rock upstarts such as Bob Dylan than he was with the Nashville establishment. It took more than thirty years for his performance at the 1964 Newport Folk Festival to be released, finally surfacing on the *Man in Black: 1963-69 Plus* box set, but it would prove to be a pivotal event in Cash's career. He performed Dylan's "Don't Think Twice, It's All Right," which he later recast as "Understand Your Man." Backstage, he met the song's author, whose reputation as a protest singer was anathema to many country fans. Cash nonetheless devoted one quarter of *Orange Blossom Special* to his new friend's compositions, including a duet with June Carter on "It Ain't Me, Babe," which reprised the Mexican brass of "Ring of Fire." Though Cash's stolid voice wasn't particularly well-equipped to handle the slippery phrasing of Dylan's songs, performing them was a bold gesture. Cash's own unequivocal civil rights commentary, "All God's Children Ain't Free," stirred controversy of its own among some country fans.

*Carryin' On*, a compilation of duets with June Carter, marks the end of Cash's relationship with producer Don Law, who resigned from Columbia before its release. The undeniable Cash-Carter rapport doesn't always translate into stellar music making; they never should have attempted Ray Charles' "What'd I Say," which finds both out of their league as would-be soul singers. But Carter growls and scolds playfully and brings out a friskier side of Cash that isn't always apparent on his solo recordings. The feistiness of "Jackson" is undeniable, a bookend to "Ring of Fire" that addresses a once-feverish love affair winding down. Cash and Carter, meanwhile, never burned hotter. Six months after the album's release, they were married.

\* \* \* \* \*

FURTHER LISTENING

*Everybody Loves a Nut*
(June 1966, No. 5 country)
*The Man in Black: 1963-69 Plus*
(October 1995)

\* \* \* \* \*

Typical of Cash's contradictory nature was his decision to record Jack Clement's "The One on the Right Is on the Left" soon after the protest-oriented *Orange Blossom Special* album. The song satirizes the self-seriousness of the folk movement: "Don't go mixin' politics with the folk songs of our land." It appears on the monumentally flippant *Everybody Loves a Nut*, designed to prove that the self-serious Cash had a sense of humor.

*The Man in Black: 1963-69 Plus*, a box set on the Bear Family label, summarizes one of Cash's most volatile periods. His pill-popping abuse, the dissolution of his first marriage and a relentless work

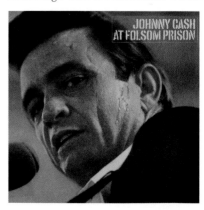

schedule led to some wildly erratic recordings. His voice deteriorated and his weight dropped precipitously. Only when he weaned himself off drugs, with June Carter Cash's help, was he able to refocus on his music and fulfill one of his fondest ambitions: to record a live album in front of a prison audience.

## THE PRISON ALBUMS 1968-69

\* \* \* \* \*

THE ESSENTIALS
"Folsom Prison Blues"
(April 1968, No. 1 country,
No. 32 pop)
*Johnny Cash at Folsom Prison*
(June 1968, No. 1 country,
No. 13 pop)
*Johnny Cash at San Quentin*
(June 1969, No. 1 country,
No. 1 pop)
"A Boy Named Sue"
(July 1969, No. 1 country,
No. 2 pop)
"San Quentin"
(July 1969)

\* \* \* \* \*

WITH "AT FOLSOM PRISON," CASH reenergized his career and cemented his reputation as a modern-day Woody Guthrie, a committed voice of the underdog. He strikes just the right balance of empathy, pathos, humor and rebellion. Cash keeps it simple: his greeting "Hello, I'm Johnny Cash," his black jacket and slacks, and no-frills arrangements that place his voice and acoustic guitar at the forefront. He has plenty of songs that speak directly to the plight of his audience — "Folsom Prison Blues," "Twenty-five Minutes to Go," "Green, Green Grass

of Home" — and balances them with a well-received sprinkling of zaniness ("Dirty Old Egg-Sucking Dog," "Flushed From the Bathroom of Your Heart"). Cash sounds utterly at ease in an environment that would have intimidated most singers. *At Folsom Prison* isn't just one of Cash's best albums, it's one of the best live albums ever made and a country music landmark. It reestablished Cash as a major figure in American music and lingered on the country charts for longer than two years.

The follow-up, *Johnny Cash at San Quentin*, recorded thirteen months later, had an even bigger impact on the pop and country charts. Cash's voice is a bit hoarse, but he compensates with a snarling intensity, cut with salty humor that the inmates boisterously encourage. His set ranges across his career, from Sun classics such as "Big River" (included on the reissue) and "I Walk the Line" to a handful of new songs, including a potent and timely interpretation of yet another Dylan tune, "Wanted Man." Tennessee Three cornerstone Luther Perkins died in August 1968, but his replacement, Bob Wootton, has already mastered his predecessor's understated, rhythm-based picking, and would remain with Cash till the end of the singer's life. Cash performs Shel Silverstein's "A Boy Named Sue" for the first time, a novelty that became Cash's biggest pop hit and kept the *San Quentin* album on the charts for seventy weeks. It arrives as comic relief after Cash has performed the newly penned "San Quentin," in which he assumes the voice of an inmate: "San Quentin, you've been living hell to me." Cash plays the song twice, and the reaction is cathartic; it sounds like a jailbreak is about to commence, but Cash keeps on entertaining the audience rather than inciting it. Later he would tell journalist Bill Flanagan that "I knew I had that prison audience where all I had to do was say, 'Take over! Break!' and they would have. Those guards knew it too. I was tempted."

## COUNTRY SUPERSTAR 1969-1971

❋ ❋ ❋ ❋ ❋

THE ESSENTIALS

"If I Were a Carpenter"
*(December 1969, No. 2 country,*
*No. 36 pop)*
*Hello, I'm Johnny Cash*
*(January 1970, No. 1 country,*
*No. 6 pop)*
"Sunday Morning Coming Down"
*(July 1970, No. 1 country,*
*No. 46 pop)*
*Man in Black*
*(June 1971, No. 1 country)*
*Johnny Cash at*
*Madison Square Garden*
*(August 2002)*

❋ ❋ ❋ ❋ ❋

WITH BOB DYLAN

*Nashville Skyline*
*(April 1969, No. 3 pop)*

❋ ❋ ❋ ❋ ❋

AMID THE HUGE COMMERCIAL SUC-cesses of Cash's one-two punch of prison albums, the Number One pop hit "A Boy Named Sue," a *Life* magazine cover story and a national television show, his 1969 concert at Madison Square Garden affirmed his stature as an artist, entertainer and storyteller who transcended musical boundaries and generations. On *Johnny Cash at*

*Madison Square Garden*, released more than thirty years after the event, Cash presides with easygoing grace over a briskly paced revue-style performance in front of a capacity audience. It lacks the explosive peaks and charged atmosphere of the prison concerts, but *Madison Square Garden* serves as a fine overview of Cash's music and influences to that point in his career. He shares time with Carl Perkins, the Carter Family and the Statler Brothers, even briefly dueting with his brother Tommy Cash on "Do What You Do, Do Well." Notable for her absence is June Carter Cash, who's back home pregnant with their son, John Carter Cash.

*Hello, I'm Johnny Cash* became Cash's third album to crack the upper reaches of the pop chart, pushed by the success of another folk-oriented duet with June, "If I Were a Carpenter." Johnny also had a major hit with the single "Sunday Morning Coming Down," by a then-unknown Kris Kristofferson. Cash cuts through the lush orchestration with his measured reading of Kristofferson's lyric about a melancholic drunk. No one else but Cash could have taken a line such as "I'm wishin', Lord, that I was stoned" to the top of the country chart.

The *Man in Black* title song is Cash's manifesto, the kind of statement that coming from almost anybody else would be laughable. But the singer's assertion that he won't retire his trademark outfit until a world of injustice is made "right" rings true – the Man in Black did indeed walk the walk. The album also includes "Singin' in Vietnam Talkin' Blues," in which Cash recounts in vivid detail his visit overseas with June ("The bullets and the bombs and the mortar shells/Shook our bed every time one fell") and concludes with an emphatic wish that the war be brought to a swift end.

During this period, Cash also recorded with Bob Dylan in Nashville. One of their ragged but heartfelt duets, "Girl From the North Country," surfaced on Dylan's *Nashville Skyline*, released in 1969. It's as close to pure country music as Dylan ever came, and it helped open the gates to the country rock of the Seventies.

## THE END OF THE COLUMBIA ERA 1972-1986

❋ ❋ ❋ ❋ ❋

THE ESSENTIALS

"Ghost Riders in the Sky"
*(May 1979, No. 2 country)*
*Silver*
*(August 1979, No. 28 country)*
*Rockabilly Blues*
*(June 1980)*
*Johnny 99*
*(September 1983)*

❋ ❋ ❋ ❋ ❋

THROUGH THE SEVENTIES, CASH'S dominance of the country charts began to erode; after a few years of indifferent recordings, he re-energized his music by working with new collaborators and recorded a handful of unjustly overlooked albums. *Silver* pairs Cash with Emmylou Harris producer Brian Ahern for a relatively experimental outing with a gaggle of sidemen and liberal sprinklings of brass and keyboards; its triumph is an atmospheric, Ennio Morricone-like version of "Ghost Riders in the Sky." It also includes a cover of son-in-law Rodney Crowell's "Bull Rider," a lyric perfectly suited to Cash's dramatic storytelling style, with Ricky Skaggs' fiddle shading the master's voice. "I'm Gonna Sit On the Porch and Pick On My Old Guitar" wraps up one of Cash's most accomplished studio recordings with a hammock-swinging grace note.

*Rockabilly Blues* is also among Cash's best later albums for Columbia; it's not rockabilly so much as an

update of the bluesy "Big River" side of his Sun Records repertoire, with an assist from another musician son-in-law, British New Wave star Nick Lowe. A similarly unadorned approach makes *Johnny 99* a keeper, with Cash covering two songs from Bruce Springsteen's recently released album *Nebraska*. Both "Johnny 99" and "Highway Patrolman" are the

types of songs Cash himself might have written, and they perfectly suit his brooding delivery.

FURTHER LISTENING
*The Gospel Road*
(April 1973, No. 12 country)
*Ragged Old Flag*
(April 1974, No. 16 country)
*One Piece at a Time*
(May 1976, No. 2 country)
*Survivors Live*
(April 1982, No. 21 country)
*Heroes*
(May 1986, No. 14 country)

✳ ✳ ✳ ✳ ✳

The two-disc *Gospel Road*, the soundtrack for a film scripted by Cash and shot during a visit to Israel, is the singer's most ambitious statement about his spiritual beliefs, filled with pious music and dialogue excerpts. The music didn't get radio play, and Cash never returned to the material in his live shows. The title song of *Ragged Old Flag* is among Cash's most sentimental American history songs, a spoken-word tribute that vilifies flag-burning protesters during the Vietnam War ("In her own good land here she's been abused"). Though the album is otherwise unremarkable, "Ragged Old Flag" had a long shelf life: Cash performed it in Washington, D.C., at a performance at Ford's Theatre attended by Ronald Reagan, and rereleased the song in 1989 when the U.S. Supreme Court decided that flag burning was "symbolic speech" protected by the First Amendment.

The title song of *One Piece at a Time* was Cash's highest-charting hit in five years and his first Top Ten song

in three years, Number One on the country charts in 1976. It's a humorous hillbilly talking blues — even slipping in some then-fashionable trucker lingo — about a factory worker who builds his own "psychobilly Cadillac" with stolen gear.

*The Survivors* documents a 1981 German concert at which Cash was joined by Jerry Lee Lewis and Carl Perkins. Three-quarters of the Million Dollar Quartet have an unrehearsed good time, running through everything from the gospel standard "Peace in the Valley" to Hank Williams' "I Saw the Light," with Lewis in particular ripping it up on the piano. Cash closed out his Columbia years with *Heroes*, accompanied by his old friend Waylon Jennings for an entire album of duets. The production by Chips Moman sweetens the gruff voices without overwhelming them, and "Even Cowgirls Get the Blues," one of two contributions from songwriter Rodney Crowell, was a modest hit, Cash's last for the label.

## THE HIGHWAYMEN 1985-99

THE ESSENTIALS
"Highwayman"
(May 1985, No. 1 country)
*Highwayman*
(May 1985, No. 1 country)

✳ ✳ ✳ ✳ ✳

CASH'S REBEL PERSONA, AND HIS affection for songs about inmates and gunslingers, helped sow the seeds for the "outlaw country" movement of the Seventies. Among the most commercially successful of the outlaws were Willie Nelson, Waylon Jennings and Kris Kristofferson — singer-song-writers who cut against the grain of the increasingly slick pop-country productions coming out of Nashville, scoring hits with songs that played up their outsider status. This success led to their union with Cash — a friend, mentor and hero to all of them in varying degrees — as a country supergroup, the Highwaymen. The timing couldn't have been better for Cash, who had virtually dropped off the country charts as his Columbia Records tenure wound down. The Jimmy Webb title song of the debut album rectified that situation, becoming Cash's first Number One country song since 1976. The production, by Chips Moman, is slick but unobtrusive, generally giving the voices plenty of room to ply lyrics that cast them as mystical cowboys drifting through time ("Highway-man") or "Desperadoes Waiting for a Train." A cool curiosity is the inclusion of a fourth, previously unheard verse to "Big River" that accommodates the four voices.

❋ ❋ ❋ ❋ ❋ ❋

FURTHER LISTENING
*Highwayman 2*
*(February 1990, No. 4 country)*
*The Road Goes On Forever*
*(April 1995, No. 42 country)*
*Super Hits*
*(March 1999)*

❋ ❋ ❋ ❋ ❋ ❋

Cash and Co. tried to repeat the *High-wayman* formula, with diminishing returns. *Highwayman 2* kicks off with "Silver Stallion," another stab at Old West mythmaking similar to the first album's title song. The most personal moment is Cash's "Songs That Make a Difference," about a 1969 session at his

house that included Bob Dylan, Joni Mitchell and Graham Nash.

## THE MERCURY YEARS 1986-1992

❋ ❋ ❋ ❋ ❋

THE ESSENTIALS
*Water From the Wells of Home*
*(November 1988, No. 48 country)*
*The Mystery of Life*
*(February 1991)*

❋ ❋ ❋ ❋ ❋

AT AGE FIFTY-FOUR AND WITHOUT a recording contract for the first time in more than thirty years, Cash was reduced to pitching his songs on Music Row in Nashville. He hardly needed the work; his considerable property holdings and publishing royalties ensured that he could have comfortably retired. But he still burned to record. He was eventually offered a modest deal on Mercury/Polygram, with the idea that he would be reunited with his old Sun Records producer and songwriting collaborator Jack Clement. Though generally regarded as a lost era for Cash (his Mercury albums were largely commercial stiffs), it was not for lack of trying. At least two of his albums from this period suggest that he was as engaged as ever in his music.

The best of them is *Water From the Wells of Home*, which brings in some heavy hitters to sing with Cash, including Paul and Linda McCartney, the Everly Brothers and Cash's daughter Rosanne. Occasionally, the Man in Black sounds like a sideman on his own record, but there's no denying the harmonies of Emmylou Harris on Roy Acuff's "As Long as I Live." The ode to perseverance "That Old Wheel" suits

Cash perfectly at this point in his career, and the singer jumps to it over a honking saxophone on J.J. Cale's "Calls Me the Breeze," with his son John Carter Cash adding vocals.

*The Mystery of Life* rolls out with one of Cash's best gospel-pop songs, "The

Greatest Cowboy of Them All," and accelerates into fourth gear with "I'm an Easy Rider." A pedal-steel-inflected version of a Tom T. Hall song presaged the end of his commercially disappointing Mercury tenure: "I'll Go Somewhere and Sing My Song Again."

❋ ❋ ❋ ❋ ❋ ❋

FURTHER LISTENING
*Johnny Cash Is Coming to Town*
*(April 1987, No. 36 country)*
*Boom Chicka Boom*
*(March 1990)*

❋ ❋ ❋ ❋ ❋ ❋

On *Johnny Cash Is Coming to Town*, Cash kicks off his Mercury era with an Elvis Costello song, the hangover blues "The Big Light," which Clement spices with horns. Nothing else on the album is quite as adventurous, however. "Back to Basics" is the headline over Cash's liner notes for *Boom Chicka Boom*, and the relatively unadorned production is a conscious throwback to the early days of the Tennessee Two. But the songs aren't particularly ambitious; "A Backstage Pass," for example, recounts the behind-the-scenes shenanigans at a Highwaymen concert, where "Whackos and weirdos, dingbats and dodos" hang out.

## THE COMEBACK 1994-2003

* * * * * *

THE ESSENTIALS

*American Recordings*
(April 1994, No. 23 country)
*Unchained*
(November 1996, No. 26 country)
*American III: Solitary Man*
(October 2000, No. 11 country)
*American IV:*
*The Man Comes Around*
(November 2002, No. 2 country,
No. 22, Billboard 200)
*"Hurt"*
(April 2003, No. 2 country,
No. 33 modern rock)
*Unearthed*
(November 2003, No. 33 country)

* * * * * *

**B**Y THE EARLY NINETIES, CASH was a nonentity in Nashville. But for a younger generation of rock artists, he remained an icon. U2 wrote a song for him, "The Wanderer," and invited him to sing it on their 1993 *Zooropa* album. Then producer Rick Rubin, who'd previously worked with such rap and metal groups as the Beastie Boys and Slayer, approached Cash about a record deal. In the final decade of Cash's life, they released four studio albums that revived the singer's career, plus three albums' worth of outtakes included on the posthumous *Unearthed* box set. It's telling that they chose to open their first album together, *American Recordings*, with "Delia's Gone," a

brutal murder ballad in the tradition of Cash's most badass songs. Rubin also gave Cash the license to sing stripped-down gospel songs and to lay bare his deepest insecurities and regrets, while introducing him to a wide range of contemporary songs and artists. What made the *American* sessions work was the singer's conviction; he made songs by Beck and Soundgarden sound of a piece with those of the Louvin Brothers and Jimmie Rodgers. Nothing was off the table, and Cash appreciated it; he himself said he hadn't been this free as an artist since his Sun Records days.

In his previous four decades, Cash had never made an album quite like *American Recordings*: alone with his acoustic guitar, ruminating on sin and redemption. The album lives up to its title because Cash's sense of drama is founded on understatement, his baritone never straining or resorting to histrionics. It's the one constant in the

quagmire of humor and bloodshed, pathos and treachery evoked by these songs, whether written by Cash or a ringer (among them Leonard Cohen and Loudon Wainwright III, whose respective contributions, "Bird on a Wire" and "The Man Who Couldn't Cry," are the album's peaks).

On *Unchained*, Cash and Rubin en-

CASH IN 2003, *back at work in the studio days after June Carter Cash passed away*

list backing musicians, but not the usual Nashville suspects. Instead, Tom Petty and the Heartbreakers play on most of the songs, with assists from the Red Hot Chili Peppers' Flea and Fleetwood Mac's Lindsey Buckingham and Mick Fleetwood. Cash adds a third verse to his Sun Records-era song "Mean Eyed Cat," and the Heartbreakers kick up some rockabilly dust. Cash makes Petty's "Southern Accents" his own – "I got my own way of working," indeed – and pours himself into "Spiritual" with an ardor that will raise goose bumps.

On *American III: Solitary Man*, a few cracks begin to appear on the proud surface of Cash's Mount Rushmore voice, especially on a cover of Petty's "I Won't Back Down." But the song defines the album, and Cash's defiance. He invests the songs with biblical gravity, particularly Nick Cave's death row chiller "The Mercy Seat."

*The Man Comes Around* introduced Cash to an MTV audience with his interpretation of Nine Inch Nails' "Hurt" and its accompanying award-winning video. The singer's performance is understated, dignified, sobering. The song couldn't be more sparse, little more than a one-handed piano chord pounding like a drum while Cash strides with funereal deliberation through a minefield of recrimination. It was a final illustration of what made Cash special: stark, simple music and emotional complexity. The years of debilitating illness have apparently taken their toll on his voice, but the wear and tear suits the subject

matter, which is preoccupied with death and the afterlife. The title track finds Cash still at the peak of his song-writing powers, writing his own Book of Revelation over a percussive acoustic guitar. He signs off with "We'll Meet Again," the devastating sadness cushioned by the presence of "The Whole Cash Gang" on backing vocals and longtime producer Jack Clement on acoustic guitar.

The outtakes collected on *Unearthed* would have constituted strong albums in themselves. The folk, country, rock, gospel and even reggae tunes Cash recorded in his last years are a testament to his endless curiosity, his tenacity not just in tolerating other, often opposing, points of view, but in making them part of his music. He's as convincing covering Bob Marley as he is a song from his mother's hymn book. The three discs of Rubin-produced rarities include Neil Young's "Poca-hontas," among the most adventurous songs Cash recorded in his last decade. The acid-tinged lyric tests the limits of his interpretive skills, but the singer clearly relates to its subtext: how American Indians became the doormats of the imperialist doctrine of Manifest Destiny. Mellotron orchestrations qualify "Pocahontas" as perhaps the

only outright example of psychedelia in the Cash canon. Cash even makes something of the maudlin "You'll Nev-er Walk Alone," the world-weariness in his voice and Benmont Tench's church organ turning it into a moving hymn.

The box set also includes a previ-ously unreleased album, *My Mother's Hymn Book*, in which Cash performs solo acoustic versions of the church songs from his youth. He recorded these songs in his backyard studio, accompanied only by engineer David Ferguson, and the intimacy enhances their power. Cash looks to the after-life with a mixture of acceptance and longing, an opportunity to finally embrace the serenity he knows he can never find in the secular world ("I was wretched and as vile as could be," he sings on "When He Reached Down His Hand for Me").

The box's final volume offers a fif-teen-song survey of the Rubin studio albums. Together, the five discs play like an aural autobiography, making it difficult to discern where the singer

ends and the song begins. "I wouldn't tell you what's right or what's wrong," Cash declares at the outset of volume three, "I'm just a singer of songs." To the end, he stayed true to that simple self-definition.

THE ESSENTIAL JOHNNY CASH 1955-1983" covers the cream of the singer's Sun Records output and chooses astutely from his long tenure at Columbia Records, cherry-picking key moments from his con-cept albums, touching on many of the major hits and acknowledging later-period gems such as his up-tempo cover of the Rolling Stones' "No Expectations." The more recent *Essential Johnny Cash* is skimpier, but it includes his remarkable cameo vocal on U2's "The Wanderer" and his duet with Bob Dylan on "Girl From the North Country," as well as his last Number One country hit, the title song of *Highwayman*.

On *Love, God, Murder,* Cash divides his career into three of its essential themes. The music is better covered on the *Essential* discs, but the liner notes — by June Carter Cash, Quentin Tarantino, Bono and Cash himself — provide an illuminating guide worth investigating for their own sake. They're nothing less than one man's embrace of the contradictions that make us human. As Cash writes, "At times, I'm a voice crying in the wilderness, but at times I'm right on the money and I know what I'm singing about."

# FAMILY TRADITION

**W**HEN JOHNNY CASH WED JUNE Carter in 1968, he married into country music's first family. June's aunt and uncle, A.P. and Sara Carter, along with her mother, Maybelle, founded the pioneering country act the Carter Family. June and Johnny's children have carried on the family tradition — June's daughter Carlene had a string of pop and country hits in the 1980s and 1990s, and Johnny's eldest daughter, Rosanne, continues to have a vital music career. The family also includes an array of musical "ex-son-in-laws," as June liked to call them — including Rodney Crowell (Rosanne's ex), Marty Stuart (Cindy's ex) and Nick Lowe (Carlene's ex).

Here are the key albums made by the Carter-Cash clan.

## THE CARTER FAMILY

*Sunshine in the Shadows:*
*Their Complete Victor Recordings*
*1931-1932 (1996)*
*The Carter Family on Border Radio*
*Vol. 1 (1995), Vol. 2 (1997)*
*The Carter Family: 1927-1934 (2002)*
*The Carter Family, Vol. 2:*
*1935-1941 (2003)*

**C**OUNTRY MUSIC STARTS HERE, WITH the series of tracks that the Carter Family made in the late 1920s at a portable recording studio in Bristol, Tennessee. With Sara Carter on autoharp and lead vocal, her cousin Maybelle on guitar and her husband, Alvin Pleasant "A.P." Carter, singing harmony, the Carter Family recorded more than 300 songs that remain country music's sacred text, including "Wildwood Flower," "Keep On the

Sunny Side" and "My Clinch Mountain Home."

The best introduction is the box set *The Carter Family: 1927-1934*; the performances show how the Carter Family expanded "country" music to encompass folk and gospel, murder ballads and love songs. The second volume documents an even more accomplished group, particularly Maybelle's revolutionary guitar playing; she simulates the sound of two guitars by playing with a thumb pick and two finger picks.

## JUNE CARTER CASH

*Press On (April 1999)*
*Wildwood Flower (September 2003)*

**T**HOUGH SHE RARELY MADE SOLO albums, June went into the studio with determination at the end of her life — making two records that are relaxed, reflective and full of her quirky personality. A folk band including Norman Blake, Crowell and Stuart backs Carter at her most unfettered on *Press On*. She recasts "Ring of Fire" as a campfire folk tune, and in "Tiffany Anastasia Lowe," she cracks herself up warning her granddaughter away from Quentin Tarantino. *Wildwood Flower* is June's answer to Johnny's *Man Comes Around*: Her voice is frayed with age, and the performances are all shaded by the nearness of death.

## CARLENE CARTER

*Blue Nun (1981)*
*I Fell in Love (1990)*
*Little Acts of Treason (1995)*

**C**ARLENE CARTER SPLIT FROM HER stepfather's touring band in the late Seventies and began doing her own brassy, roots-rocking songs as well as

Elvis Costello and Graham Parker covers; in 1979 she married U.K. singer-songwriter Nick Lowe. That British New Wave influence is heard on *Blue Nun*, her best early record. After a long hiatus, she came back strong with help from Howie Epstein (her then-boyfriend) and Benmont Tench of Tom Petty's Heartbreakers. She brings it all the way home on *Little Acts of Treason*, with guest appearances by Johnny and June and Carlene's father, Carl Smith.

## ROSANNE CASH

*Seven Year Ache (1981)*
*King's Record Shop (1988)*
*Interiors (1990)*
*Retrospective (1995)*
*Rules of Travel (2003)*

**A**FTER WORKING AS A TEENAGE BACK-up singer for her father, Rosanne Cash forged her own idiosyncratic sound, making her one of the greatest young singer-songwriters of 1980s. Cash had her first major success with *Seven Year Ache*, produced by Crowell, which spun off three Number One country hits. The Cash-Crowell collaboration culminated with *King's Record Shop*, one of the decade's key country albums. On *Interiors*, Cash created a concept album about heartbreak. For the first time, she produced her work herself, and her sound shifted toward a more subdued but no less potent brand of folk-pop. *Rules of Travel* includes duets with Sheryl Crow, Steve Earle and, most movingly of all, Johnny Cash. "September When It Comes" finds a father bidding his daughter farewell, in search of "a place where I can rest."

# SCREEN LIFE
## CASH'S GREATEST FILM & TV MOMENTS

By
## MARK BINELLI

OHNNY CASH'S LEGACY in film and television doesn't come close to what he achieved in music. But that doesn't mean Cash's work on-screen isn't worth seeking out. His televised concert performances, of course, are the best place to start — from his earliest appearances on shows like *Town Hall Party* and *The Ed Sullivan Show* to the weekly turns on his own prime-time variety show. But the big surprise, despite all the kitschy and just plain bizarre choices attendant to any country superstar's Hollywood career, is the fact that this guy could act. This may not come as a shock to anyone who's seen Cash onstage. As with any born performer, Cash had a knack for making sure his audiences couldn't tear their eyes away.

CASH'S FILM DEBUT, *"Five Minutes to Live,"* *1961. He played vicious bank robber Johnny Cabot alongside Ron Howard and country singer Merle Travis.*

## TOWN HALL PARTY

**F**OR THE BEST FOOTAGE of Johnny Cash as young, gifted and not yet wearing black, his performances on *Town Hall Party* are essential. The long-running country & western answer to *American Bandstand, Town Hall Party* began as a live radio show in 1951. It was broadcast every Saturday night from a theater in the Compton neighborhood of Los Angeles, its set designed to simulate a barn dance. Cash and the Tennessee Two appeared in November 1958 and again in August 1959, both times turning out riveting performances of early hits, from straight-up rockabilly numbers like "Get Rhythm" to the ballad "Give My Love to Rose" and the furious twang of "I Got Stripes." The Tennessee Two can be seen flanking Cash in counterpoint: Marshall Grant wildly slapping

*"THE MAN, HIS WORLD, His Music," with June, 1969. The documentary captured Cash at the height of his career, in performances and rare private moments.*

his stand-up bass, while gaunt guitarist Luther Perkins stands creepy and nearly immobile, occasionally glancing at his boss out of the corner of his eye, as if awaiting a signal to start taking hostages and killing people. (Introducing Perkins, Cash jokes, "We haven't had the heart to tell him, but he's been dead for two years now.") Cash himself, with his jet-black pompadour and smoldering eyes, exudes an intensity that recalls Robert Mitchum's crazed preacher in *The Night of the Hunter.* In a comic high point, Cash messily combs his hair forward and does a mock-Elvis version of "Heartbreak Hotel," complete with priapic pelvis thrusting. A twenty-four-track DVD collects uncut versions of both episodes.

## FIVE MINUTES TO LIVE

**W**HEN CASH'S SUN STUDIOS contemporary Elvis Presley decided to make the leap to the big screen, he chose to play a handsome Civil War-era hero in the sweet *Love*

*Me Tender. Five Minutes to Live,* on the other hand, opens with a wild-eyed Cash machine-gunning a cop; a few scenes later, he shoots his girlfriend in cold blood while she's listening to a record. In this 1960 B movie – his Hollywood debut – Cash plays Johnny Cabot, a bank robber (and violent sociopath) hiding out in the California suburbs. He's recruited by Vic Tayback (best known in his paunchier years as Mel from the sitcom *Alice*) to take part in a perfect heist: hold a bank vice president's wife hostage and demand the vaults be opened for ransom. Cash, in charge of the kidnapping end of the scheme, poses as a door-to-door guitar-lesson salesman, allowing him to have a guitar in hand during the hostage scene for convenient title-track strumming. He also sneers quite a bit and delivers lines like "This suburb life ain't for me" and the immortal "I guess you gals is all alike when ol' Johnny steps on your starter." Cash ponied up $20,000 of his own money when the production's financing ran out midway through shooting. By certain standards, this may have been an unwise investment: The film received abysmal reviews, and, judged sheerly on "acting skill," Cash's performance leaves something to be desired. Still, *Five Minutes to Live* (also released as *Door-to-Door Maniac*) has become a cult favorite.

### JOHNNY CASH! THE MAN, HIS WORLD, HIS MUSIC

THIS 1969 DOCUMENTARY does for Cash what *Don't Look Back* did for Bob Dylan and *Gimme Shelter* did for the Rolling Stones. It's a scintillating look at an artist at the peak of his game and, for the Cash fan, a revelatory mixture of live performances and ambling behind-the-scenes footage that could be outtakes from a home movie. There's Cash hunting and serenading a crow with a broken wing that he's just shot, and recording "One Too Many Mornings" in the studio with Dylan. Cash also sings for a Native American tribe and patiently gives career advice to a guitar-playing kid backstage. But the film's choicest moments are in the details: June Carter Cash slyly referring to her husband as "ol' Golden Throat" during a prison performance and Johnny coaxing his father into warbling an old World War I song ("Johnny, I ain't no singer," insists the elder Cash). Best of all, Cash takes the camera crew on a tour of his tiny Arkansas hometown, personally driving the band RV past shotgun shacks and cotton fields as he narrates scenes from his boyhood. He walks into his childhood home, asking his sister, "Sure looks smaller, doesn't it?" Inside, she points out the spot on the floor where Cash once sat and listened to the radio while his father yelled at him to turn it down. Back in the RV, Cash notes, "I've learned to adapt very well to prosperity."

### LIVE FROM SAN QUENTIN

THE 1968 RELEASE *Johnny Cash at Folsom Prison* became one of the best-selling albums of Cash's career. For the follow-up, recorded that same year and released in 1969 to an even greater commercial response, Cash traveled to San Quentin, this time bringing along a British film crew from Granada Television. Though the album is familiar to most Cash fans, this documentary remains a companion to the set that's well worth seeking out. It's thrilling to see Cash and his band in prison blue – they wore outfits the same color as the prisoners' as an act of solidarity – confidently dispatching classics-to-be such as "San Quentin," with lines like "San Quentin, I hate every inch of you," and receiving standing ovations from the inmates. (The cons also seem to *really* dig June.) "If any of the guards are still speakin' to me," Cash asks at one point from the stage, "could I have a glass of water?"

### THE JOHNNY CASH SHOW

TAPED IN FRONT OF A LIVE AUDIENCE at Nashville's legendary Ryman Auditorium, Cash's prime-time Saturday-night variety show ran on ABC from 1969 to 1971. The show debuted at a time when country music was gaining mainstream popularity. As the writer Tom Dearmore noted in a 1969 *New York Times Magazine* profile of Cash, "Indeed the country seems to have gone 'country'-crazy: *The Beverly Hillbillies* goes on and on, *Hee Haw* is a Sunday prime-time prize of CBS's and 'country' singers have now 'made the networks' with their own shows." But *The Johnny Cash Show* was a far cry from that cornpone fare. Cash's musical guests on his debut episode include Joni Mitchell and Bob Dylan. The stage sets are awful, seemingly borrowed from the *Lawrence Welk Show* prop closet, but the performances more than redeem such aesthetic shortcomings. Mitchell sits beside Cash on a fake stone wall to duet on the lovely "I Still Miss Someone," while Dylan, after a solo rendition of "I Threw It All Away," joins Cash for their *Nashville Skyline* duet, "Girl From the North Country." That first episode also opens with a hilariously mod title sequence, featuring "Folsom Prison Blues" redone as an *Austin Powers*-era instrumental. Later

after his horse dies. He eventually meets Douglas, the local desperado – who has also seen better days – and the two agree to shoot it out to the death in a bullring while a crowd of locals bets and cheers. The film was well-received, with *Today's Cinema* noting that "the big surprise of the film is the assurance with which singer Johnny Cash handles the demanding role of Abe Cross."

## THE GOSPEL ROAD

POSSIBLY THE WEIRDEST ARTIFACT from an impressively weird film and television career, this 1973 retelling of the life of Jesus was co-produced, scored, co-written and narrated by Cash. His old friend Robert Elfstrom (director of *Johnny Cash! The Man, His World, His Music*) directed and – in what most agree to be the worst biblical casting since Charles Heston hefted the Ten Commandments – starred as Christ himself, which seems a tad misguided, as Elfstrom is blond, beefy and Scandinavian. (Reviews of the film note that Elfstrom can actually be seen squinting uncomfortably in the desert sunlight.) Otherwise, the director takes a documentary approach to the film, using hand-held cameras and nonactors – including June Carter Cash as Mary Magdalene. Cash himself occasionally ambles onscreen, dressed head-to-toe in black as he tells the story of the Gospel beside the Sea of Galilee.

## RIDIN' THE RAILS

BACK IN THE LEAN YEARS of the 1930s, Cash's father was forced to hop freight trains in order to get away from the family farm and find work elsewhere. This fact may

*OPPOSITE: KIRK DOUGLAS recruited Cash for the starring role in 1971's "A Gunfight." ABOVE: "The Last Days of Frank and Jesse James," with Kris Kristofferson, 1986.*

shows would feature Neil Young, Stevie Wonder, James Taylor, Derek and the Dominos, the Guess Who, Ray Charles, Roy Orbison and the occasional nonmusical guest like Dennis Hopper or Albert Brooks, alongside country artists such as Merle Haggard, Tammy Wynette, Waylon Jennings and Hank Williams Jr. In a special college episode filmed at Vanderbilt University in Nashville, Young performs "Needle and the Damage Done," and Cash premieres a song he wrote especially for the episode, "The Man in Black." He also tapes remote segments in which he answers questions from various students on the campus grounds. (Cash, surrounded by hippies, wears the sort of full-length fur coat that had been the college fashion several decades earlier.) When one student asks if there is a problem with drugs in the music industry, Cash replies, "Well, there was in this end of the music industry."

### A GUNFIGHT

KIRK DOUGLAS personally recruited Cash to star opposite him in this 1971 Western. Cash plays an aging gunfighter stranded in a small town

*FROM LEFT: JANE SEYmour, Johnny Cash and June Carter Cash, on the set of "Dr. Quinn, Medicine Woman," 1993*

CASH PLAYED A *scheming country star* on "Columbo" in 1974.

partly explain Cash's lifelong obsession with the loco-motive. On his prime-time variety show, he had a regular segment called "Ride This Train," in which he would speak and sing about the plight of Native Americans and steel-driving legends like John Henry from a set made to look like an old train depot. In this 1975 television docu-mentary, filmed in twenty-five days on twelve locations, Cash leads the viewer as the onscreen narrator. There are reenactments of a race between a horse and a steam engine as well as the driving of the golden spike, while Cash schools us about Casey Jones and the dramatic battle over the Civil War locomotive the General. Toward the end of the special, Cash boards a modern-day train and serenades sleepy and confused-looking passengers with "City of New Orleans." All together now: *Good morning, America, how arrrrre you?*

## COLUMBO

CASH MADE GUEST APPEARANCES as an actor on a number of television series, including *Little House on the Prairie* (he played a confidence man posing as a preacher), *Dr. Quinn, Medicine Woman* (as the cowboy gunslinger Kid Cole) and *The Muppet Show* (singing "Ghost Riders in the Sky," a train-song medley and a tense duet of "Dirty Old Egg-Sucking Dog" with Rolf, the piano-playing dog). Still, Cash's greatest TV guest shot has to be his turn on a 1974 episode of *Columbo* called "Swan Song," in which he plays Tommy Brown, a gospel-singing country superstar who decides to off his holy-roller wife in the most insane way possible: While flying his private plane from Bakersfield, California, to Los Angeles, he drugs his

wife's coffee, parachutes from the plane and then pretends he was thrown from the crash and miracu-lously survived. Shortsightedly after such an elaborate plan, he doesn't bother to destroy the parachute, instead hiding it under a stump near the crash site. When Columbo visits Brown's L.A. pad on the day of the funeral and finds him poolside, playing his guitar to bikini-clad starlets and feasting on squirrel-meat chili, you know Peter Falk's not putting away his crumpled notepad until he finds that parachute.

## TV MOVIES

PERHAPS DUE TO the somewhat marginalized nature of the country superstar within the wider realm of popular culture, Cash made very few feature films, despite the success of *A Gunfight.* He did grace a rather dismaying number of made-for-television movies with his presence going back as early as the 1970, with the retelling of the forced Cherokee migration *Trail of Tears.* In 1978, he played a drunk hell-raiser who finds redemption after buying a Texas citrus farm in *Thaddeus Rose and Eddie;* in 1981, an adult struggling with illiteracy in *The Pride of Jesse Hallam;* in 1985, the radical abolitionist John Brown in the Civil War miniseries *North and South.* Then, after the success of Kenny Rogers' TV-movie version of *The Gam-bler,* a microgenre was spawned: the country-star TV West-ern. Cash appeared in two: a 1986 remake of the John Ford–John Wayne classic *Stagecoach,* co-starring Willie Nelson, Kris Kristofferson, Waylon Jennings and *Dukes of Hazzard* heartthrob John Schneider, and, that same year, *The Last Days of Frank and Jesse James,* with Cash as Frank (wearing costumes from John Wayne's old wardrobe), Kristoffer-son as Jesse and supporting turns from Nelson and David Allan Coe. In the end, the most interesting facet of Cash's TV-movie career arguably happened off-camera: While in Georgia filming the 1983 movie *Murder in Coweta County,* an attempt was allegedly made on his life when someone cut the brake hose on a '48 Ford he'd been set to drive.

## MUSIC VIDEOS

CASH MADE HIS FIRST FORMAL MUSIC VIDEO in 1976, when he filmed a strange clip for his novelty hit "One Piece at a Time," which tells the story of a line worker at

an auto plant who cobbles together a Frankenstein vehicle from five-finger-discounted parts. In the low-budget video, shot outside Cash's Tennessee home, Cash marvels at his ride, then takes a spin with June reclining in the backseat, the film often speeding up to wacky effect, à la Benny Hill or *The Monkees.* In 1984, as MTV took off, he shot another offbeat video for the otherwise forgettable "Chicken in Black" single, in which he donned a ridiculous mock-Superman outfit at various Nashville locations. It wasn't until his Rick Rubin-helmed comeback in the early Nineties that Cash made videos truly worthy of his music. For the disturbing black-and-white clip for "Delia's Gone," director Anton Corbijn cast supermodel Kate Moss as Delia. MTV balked at the result, which featured Cash tying Moss to a chair, shooting her and shoveling dirt onto her corpse. A Cash spokesman responded at the time, "I guess they have a thing about dead women. We don't quite understand their reaction."

While scouting locations for what would be Cash's final video — his 2002 cover of the Nine Inch Nails song "Hurt" — director Mark Romanek visited the House of Cash museum in Nashville. "It had been closed since the Eighties; there was water damage everywhere," Romanek recalled. "When I saw the place was in such a state of dereliction, that's when I got the idea that maybe we could be extremely candid about the state of Johnny's health — as candid about the state of Johnny's life at this moment as Johnny has always been in his songs." The result became one of the most intense and affecting videos in the history of MTV. Romanek combined shots of the museum ruins with footage of Cash yesterday and today — dashing archival images of the young Man in

ABOVE: IN 1970's *"Trail of Tears," Cash played a Cherokee chief.* LEFT: *Johnny and June starred in 1983's "Murder in Coweta County." During the filming, Cash almost died when someone cut his car's brake cables.*

Black riding trains and entertaining prisoners juxtaposed with the present-day Cash at home, with no effort made to cover up his age or frailty. "Mortality is a very unusual topic for this particular medium," Romanek said. "But I really ascribe most of the power to the Johnny Cash-ness of it all."

# REMEMBERING

## JOHNNY CASH

BOB DYLAN ∗ MERLE HAGGARD ∗ KRIS KRISTOFFERSON ∗ BONO

AL GORE ∗ JERRY LEE LEWIS ∗ MARTY STUART

EMMYLOU HARRIS ∗ MARK ROMANEK ∗ SHERYL CROW

STEVE EARLE ∗ TOM PETTY

> *"Johnny was and is the North Star; you could guide your ship by him."*

# BOB DYLAN

I WAS ASKED TO GIVE A STATEMENT on Johnny's passing and thought about writing a piece instead called "Cash Is King," because that is the way I really feel. In plain terms, Johnny was and is the North Star; you could guide your ship by him — the greatest of the greats, then and now. I first met him in '62 or '63 and saw him a lot in those years. Not so much recently, but in some kind of way he was with me more than people I see every day.

There wasn't much music media in the early Sixties, and *Sing Out!* was the magazine covering all things folk in character. The editors had published a letter chastising me for the direction my music was going. Johnny wrote the magazine back an open letter telling the editors to shut up and let me sing, that I knew what I was doing. This was before I had ever met him, and the letter meant the world to me. I've kept the magazine to this day.

Of course, I knew of him before he ever heard of me. In '55 or '56, "I Walk the Line" played all summer on the radio, and it was different from anything else you had ever heard. The record sounded like a voice from the middle of the earth. It was so powerful and moving. It was profound, and so was the tone of it, every line; deep and rich, awesome and mysterious all at once. "I Walk the Line" had a monumental presence and a certain type of majesty that was humbling. Even a simple line like "I find it very, very easy to be true" can take your measure. We can remember that and see how far we fall short of it.

Johnny wrote thousands of lines like that. Truly, he is what the land and country are all about, the heart and soul of it personified and what it means to be here; and he said it all in plain English. I think we can have recollections of him, but we can't define him any more than we can define a fountain of truth, light and beauty. If we want to know what it means to be mortal, we need look no further than the Man in Black. Blessed with a profound imagination, he used the gift to express all the various lost causes of the human soul. This is a miraculous and humbling thing. Listen to him, and he always brings you to your senses. He rises high above all, and he'll never die or be forgotten, even by persons not born yet — especially those persons — and that is forever.

> *"He was like
> Abraham or
> Moses — one
> of the great
> men who will
> ever grace
> the earth."*

# MERLE
# HAGGARD

MET JOHNNY in 1963 in a restroom in Chicago. I was taking a leak, and he walked up beside me with a flask of wine underneath his coat and said, "Haggard, you want a drink of this wine?" Those were the first words he ever said to me, but I had been in awe of him since I saw him play on New Year's Day in 1958 at San Quentin Prison, where I was an inmate. He'd lost his voice the night before over in Frisco and wasn't able to sing very good; I thought he'd had it, but he won over the prisoners. He had the right attitude: He chewed gum, looked arrogant and flipped the bird to the guards — he did everything the prisoners wanted to do. He was a mean mother from the South who was there because he loved us. When he walked away, everyone in that place had become a Johnny Cash fan. There were 5,000 inmates in San Quentin and about thirty guitar players; I was among the top five guitarists in there. The day after Johnny's show, man, every guitar player in San Quentin was after me to teach them how to play like him. It was like how, the day after a Muhammad Ali fight, everybody would be down in the yard shadowboxing; that day, everyone was trying to learn "Folsom Prison Blues." Then when my career caught fire, he asked me to be a guest on his variety show on ABC. He, June and I were discussing what I should do on the show, and he said, "Haggard, let me tell the people you've been to prison. It'll be the biggest thing that will happen to you in your life, and the tabloids will never be able to hurt you. It's called telling the truth: If you start off telling the truth, your fans never forget it." I told him, "Being an ex-convict is the most shameful thing. It's against the grain to talk about it." But he was right — it set a fire under me that hadn't been there before.

We knew he'd been sick, and we'd thought he was going to die so many times over the last couple years — if you want to get really serious, he'd been near death for decades. Johnny Cash lived in constant, serious pain: On a scale of one to ten, it was somewhere around an eight for the last eight years of his life. He dealt himself some terrible years where he didn't do the right things. He didn't eat right, so his bones got brittle; his jaw broke during some dental surgery and never healed. He lived as an example of a man in pain, going from one stage of bad health to another, but he held his head up the whole way. He was like Abraham or Moses — one of the great men who will ever grace the earth. There will never be another Man in Black.

# KRIS KRISTOFFERSON

*"He represented so much that appealed to me — like freedom."*

WAS HIS JANITOR for a year and a half at Columbia Records Studio, and I pitched John every song I ever wrote. He never cut any of them then, but he was always encouraging. He even carried one set of my lyrics around in his wallet, and at the time that was enough for me. Then when he got his television show, it was a really important phase in the development of country music here in Nashville. He brought in a lot of people who weren't normally in Nashville, like Joni Mitchell, Linda Ronstadt, James Taylor, Ray Charles. He put me on the show too, and he recorded my song "Sunday Morning Coming Down" and made it Record of the Year. I never had to work another job again.

John was my hero a long time before I ever met him. He represented so much that appealed to me — like freedom. He was willing and able to be the champion of people who didn't have one. And I think the power of his performance came from the tension between this man who was deeply spiritual and also a real wild man. I can see how rappers would love that "I shot a man in Reno" attitude. But to me, he doesn't represent danger, he represents integrity. And Jesus, that's just what we can't afford to lose today.

# BONO

*"We're all sissies in comparison to Johnny Cash."*

EVERY MAN COULD RELATE to him. But nobody could be him. To be that extraordinary and that ordinary was his real gift. That, and his humor and his bare-boned honesty. When I visited him at home one time, he said the most beautiful, poetic grace. He said, "Shall we bow our heads?" We all bowed our heads. Then, when he was done, he looked at me and Adam Clayton and said, "Sure miss the drugs, though." It was just to say, "I haven't become a holy Joe." He just couldn't be self-righteous. I think he was a very godly man, but you had the sense that he had spent his time in the desert. And that just made you like him more. It gave his songs some dust. And that voice was definitely locusts and honey. As for "Hurt," it's perhaps the best video ever made.

I was telling somebody just the other day, "We're all sissies in comparison to Johnny Cash." And he was a zookeeper, too. Did you know he was nearly killed by an emu on his property? He told me, "That emu damn near killed me. I defended myself with a post." But he was laughing as he told the story.

So Johnny Cash passed away after seeing off the love of his life. That's such a different outcome than death by emu. We should be grateful.

*"You could tell when he talked about what was going on in America that he cared most of all for those who have a tough row to hoe."*

**W**HEN I WAS ELECTED to Congress twenty-seven years ago, my district included Johnny Cash's home in Hendersonville, twenty-five minutes north of Nashville. Back then, there was only one personal connection, through June Carter Cash, whom my father had known when she was a girl performing with her legendary family on WSM radio.

As I got to know Johnny Cash the man, I loved his music much more — not for the normal reason that you appreciate the work of your friends, but because it was just obvious at close range that what made his songs so great was that the man himself was deep, deep, deep.

He had felt a lot of pain in his life (though he told me a few months ago that the worst pain he ever felt was when he lost June last May). But midway through his life, he found the strength to learn from his mistakes, acknowledge them honestly and transcend them.

And maybe because of what he had gone through, he felt a deep connection to the suffering of others. He was to the left of me on many issues; for example, he was against the death penalty. He cared about social conditions and wanted laws and policies that would help the poor and disadvantaged. You could always tell when he talked about what was going on in America that he cared most of all for those who have a tough row to hoe.

To my ears, his songs have always been beautiful, powerful and moving in a completely original way. In fact, I remember arguing with ROLLING STONE's critic who reviewed Johnny's last album with what I thought was too-faint praise. His music will grow considerably in stature as time passes. That unusually strong connection between the soul of the artist and the integrity of his art will lift it up and set it apart, and its rare beauty will be more readily recognized, because it draws its power from that shimmering link between song and soul.

# JERRY LEE LEWIS

*"John was religious-thinking, if not always religious-acting."*

**I** DID THE FIRST TOUR ever with Johnny Cash — way back in 1956. It was me, him and Carl Perkins, a thirty-day tour all the way through Canada, and there weren't any paved highways or anything, nothing but gravel roads. I remember what a great showman Johnny was. The way he sang was completely different, and he had a whole different style that he created himself. John, Elvis and them were rockabilly; I was rock & roll. But we all had country in us, which manifested itself in different ways. If you break it all down to the nitty-gritty, we're all country people. We were called rebels — I guess because we were. Whatever we took a notion to, we just did it. John was religious-thinking, if not always religious-acting. One of the most ridiculous things Johnny and I ever did was steal a television set out of a hotel; there was a little bitty television up on the wall, and we got it off. Johnny wanted it for his wife; I helped him get it, because I didn't see any reason why he shouldn't have it.

I hope when his heart quit beatin' that he was ready to meet his maker. I don't know if he was; I'm not the judge. He was a man of faith, which I think should help. I just hope he made it through the gates.

M ERLE AND I HAVE BEEN TOURING together all summer, and the first show was the first annual Merle Haggard UFO Music Fest, in Roswell, New Mexico. You'll be happy to know that Johnny Cash went to heaven with a commemorative Merle Haggard UFO Music Fest guitar pick. John would've appreciated the gesture – most people didn't know that side of him. Every December, he and I would go to the graveyard to visit Luther [Perkins, Cash's original guitarist] and bring him a cigarette. We would lie down on the grave, smoke and talk to Luther, telling him what a lazy son of a bitch he was for lying there while we were out touring, killing ourselves to promote him.

When I was in John's band during the Eighties, we were down to playing Branson, Missouri-type shows for elderly people. Nashville was done with him. Instead of giving him the respect he deserved, they treated him like a fossil. But with the *American Recordings* album, his career had a rebirth just by him doing what the fuck he wanted to do. He had a brand-new audience, which put wind in his sail. He wasn't having to do his old patriotic Johnny Cash tricks for a bunch of older Americans; it was kids with tattoos and weird hair trying to find their way.

I don't think he was scared of things. I don't think he was scared of death or illness – he'd been through all that. I saw him have to go to the Betty Ford clinic after a farm animal punctured his stomach. He went back on painkillers, and with us addicts, all it takes is one pill to set us back. But I think he was scared most of losing people – he lost his mom, his dad, his wife – and of the dark force of Satan. John fully understood the power of the dark force. He'd be on his knees with a Bible in his hands, trying to cope with his demons. He believed what he read in the Bible and tried to practice it.

*"You'll be happy to know that Johnny Cash went to heaven with a Merle Haggard UFO Music Fest guitar pick."*

# EMMYLOU HARRIS

*"He seemed to be the voice of truth in everything he did."*

**I** WAS DOING A SHOW with Neil Young in Nashville just after Johnny died. Before the show, Neil was telling me how sorry he was about Johnny. And at the end of "Rockin' in the Free World," Neil played "Taps" on the guitar. It was beautiful.

John seemed so completely American, if I may say that in a time of such turmoil that I'm not sure we know who we are as a people. He seemed to be the voice of truth in everything he did. There was nothing unnatural about John Cash — this was not an act. He rose to the occasion on *The Man Comes Around* in a way that was astonishing. And the video they made of "Hurt" puts all those bare-navel, soft-porn videos to shame. It shows videos can actually have a profound effect on us, and it took Johnny Cash to once again show that. It's come full circle, because when he first came on the scene with that power, he was all that rock & roll could be.

T HE SADNESS IN THE VIDEO is genuine. Johnny said that "Hurt" was the best anti-drug song he'd ever heard. The rage you see when he pours the wine on the table or starts to weep is a direct result of having lost people to addictions — and almost having lost himself. But he was playing a role. On set, when we yelled, "Cut," a very different, very funny, much more energetic Johnny Cash emerged. When we were shooting the piano scene, he said, "Maybe you want June to dance naked on the piano there." June said, "Oh, John!" and the crew broke up. He was playful with June — the degree to which they were in love with each other was palpable after all these years. Johnny was also extremely generous — he autographed about thirty-five vinyl copies of *The Man Comes Around* as a parting gift to the crew, who were in awe. That had never been done by any of the forty artists I've worked with.

# MARK ROMANEK

VIDEO DIRECTOR, "HURT"

*"He was playful with June — the degree to which they were in love with each other was palpable after all these years."*

# SHERYL CROW

*"John represented
the salt of the earth to me."*

I SANG AT JOHN'S FUNERAL, and I cannot lie: It was very hard. There was a real sense we had turned a corner. Because there can never be another Johnny Cash. I grew up in a place where people were very God-fearing, land-loving, and John represented the salt of the earth to me. He spoke for every man and personified the human struggles that we all go through. He was almost biblical, because he walked this earth and experienced all a man could suffer. Yet he still rose up out of the ashes with this great strength and gave voice to that strength for all of us.

*"When I was locked up, he sent me a letter saying how everybody was pulling for me."*

## STEVE EARLE

OHNNY WAS ONE OF THE FEW PEOPLE who wrote me when I was locked up — he sent me a very encouraging letter saying how everybody was pulling for me, that he and June were praying for me and that he would see me when I got out. I saw him again when I helped put together the band for his song on the *Dead Man Walking* soundtrack. When I got to the studio, nobody was there but John and the engineer. I walk in and there's this old-fashioned picnic basket sitting in the middle of the pool table — you know, gingham tablecloth, the whole bit. John's got his hand in that picnic basket, and he looks up and says, "Steve, would you like a piece of tenderloin on a biscuit that June made this morning?" I was really hungry, so I said, "Yeah," and he said, "I knew you would." We could've talked about our shared demons — I'd been clean probably a year and a half — but he knew that sometimes it's better to leave some things private and just talk about tenderloin and biscuits.

# TOM PETTY

THE FIRST TIME I MET JOHN was in 1982. I was with Nick Lowe, who was his son-in-law at the time, and we were in Nashville. John invited us to have a meal at his place out on the lake. We arrived, but we were disappointed, because John had taken ill that morning and had gone to the hospital with pneumonia — him and June. But the meal was still going to go on. We sat at this long, elaborately set table. Just as the meal was about to begin, someone said, "Tom, John's on the phone and would like to talk to you." So I went to the phone, and we talked for, God, about half an hour. Then after dinner, he and June spoke to every single guest by phone as they left the house and asked if they had a good time. When John came out to Los Angeles to make *Unchained*, me and the Heartbreakers kind of became his band. I still view that as the best work we ever did. One of my favorite stories is being at this studio in downtown Hollywood — which is kind of a weird neighborhood — when John came in with June. He was laughing, so I said, "Hey, where you been?" He said, "June and I thought it would be fun to just sit on that bus bench across the street for a while. I met the most interesting people over there." I said, "You're kidding me." I was trying to picture the look on these people's faces as they came to wait for the bus and there's Johnny and June. This guy was friends with presidents, and he was friends with people at the bus stop.

*"This guy was friends with presidents, and he was friends with people at the bus stop."*

## ACKNOWLEDGEMENTS

WE ARE INDEBTED TO MANY PEOPLE for making this book special. We are grateful to Johnny Cash's children – Cindy Cash, Rosanne Cash, Tara Cash Schwoebel, Kathy Cash Tittle and John Carter Cash – for their generous contributions of family photos and recollections of their father. To Jann S. Wenner, for his guidance and support, and for making this book possible. To Lou Robin, Cash's longtime manager and friend, for his indispensable assistance. And to ROLLING STONE deputy managing editor Joe Levy for his insight and careful editing. To Jim Flammia at Lost Highway, Tom Cording at Sony/Legacy and to the Museum of Television & Radio, for providing access to their abundant resources. We also thank Carrie Thornton, Jason Gordon, Mark McCauslin and Felix Gregorio at Crown Publishers; our agent, Sarah Lazin, for her hard work and advice; and Gary Montalvo, Darren Cox and Taylor Gillis at SpotCo, who helped put the book together. Thanks to Evelyn Bernal, our business manager, and her assistants, Barbara Slavin and Maureen Lamberti. And to our colleagues at ROLLING STONE who gave their time and effort: Tom Nawrocki, Ed Needham, Nathan Brackett, Jennifer Santana, Rex Robinson, Kara Brandenstein, John Dragonetti and Paul Leung; and interns Stephen Marzolf, Frederick Deknatel and Janice Schiffman. To Jon Langford, for the amazing painting; and to David Wild and Matt Diehl, who conducted interviews. Finally, thank you to Johnny Cash, for the way your music and your life have touched us all and made us better people.
—JASON FINE

# CONTRIBUTORS

### MARK BINELLI
*Mark Binelli is a contributing editor at* Rolling Stone.

### ROSANNE CASH
*Rosanne Cash is Johnny Cash's eldest daughter, as well as an author, songwriter and recording artist. Her latest album, "Black Cadillac," will be released in 2004.*

### ANTHONY DeCURTIS
*Anthony DeCurtis is a* Rolling Stone *contributing editor, the executive editor of "Tracks" and the author of "Rocking My Life Away: Writing About Music and Other Matters." He has won a Grammy Award for Best Album Notes, and he teaches in the writing program at the University of Pennsylvania.*

### JANCEE DUNN
*Jancee Dunn is a contributing editor at* Rolling Stone. *She has been with the magazine since 1989.*

### JASON FINE
*Jason Fine is an assistant managing editor at* Rolling Stone, *where he has worked since 1997. He edited the 2002 book "Harrison," a* Rolling Stone *tribute to George Harrison.*

### DAVID FRICKE
*David Fricke has been writing for* Rolling Stone *since the late Seventies and has been on staff since 1985; he is currently a senior editor. He is a three-time winner of the ASCAP-Deems Taylor Award and has written liner notes for CD reissues by the Byrds, the Ramones, Moby Grape and many others.*

### MIKAL GILMORE
*Mikal Gilmore is a* Rolling Stone *contributing editor and has been writing for the magazine since 1976. He is also the author of "Night Beat: A Shadow History of Rock & Roll" and the auto-biographical "Shot in the Heart," recently adapted to film for HBO.*

### RALPH J. GLEASON
*Ralph J. Gleason co-founded* Rolling Stone *with editor Jann S. Wenner in 1967. He was a contributing editor until he passed away in 1975 at the age of fifty-eight.*

### ROBERT HILBURN
*Robert Hilburn, former contributor to* Rolling Stone *and author of a biography of Bruce Springsteen for Rolling Stone Press, is the pop music critic and pop music editor at the "Los Angeles Times."*

### GREG KOT
*Greg Kot is the music critic for the "Chicago Tribune," the co-host of radio talk show "Sound Opinions" and a frequent contributor to* Rolling Stone. *His book "Wilco: Learning How to Die" will be published in 2004.*

### STEVE POND
*Steve Pond began writing for* Rolling Stone *in 1979 and was an associate editor and contributing editor at the magazine for more than twelve years.*

# PHOTOGRAPHY CREDITS

PAGE 5: Danny Clinch/Corbis Outline. PAGES 8-9: Courtesy of Don Hunstein/Sony. PAGE 11: Courtesy of Rosanne Cash. PAGE 15: Photofest. PAGE 17: Showtime Archives, Toronto. PAGE 19: Ruven Afanador/Corbis Outline. PAGE 20: Courtesy of Don Hunstein/Sony. PAGE 23: Courtesy of Don Hunstein/Sony. PAGE 24: Photofest. PAGE 25: Courtesy of Tara Cash Schwoebel. PAGE 26: Michael Ochs Archives. PAGES 28-29: Michael Ochs Archives. PAGE 31: Courtesy of Don Hunstein/Sony. PAGE 33: Courtesy of Rosanne Cash. PAGE 36: Courtesy of Bob Cato/Sony. PAGE 39, TOP: Courtesy of Bob Cato/Sony. PAGE 39, BOTTOM: Courtesy of Tara Cash Schwoebel. PAGE 41: ©Jim Marshall. PAGE 42: Frank Driggs Collection/Getty Images. PAGES 44-45: J.T. Phillips/Globe Photos. PAGES 48-49: Christopher Little/Corbis Outline. PAGE 51: Mark Seliger/Corbis Outline. PAGE 52: Courtesy of John Carter Cash. PAGE 55: Martin Schoeller/Corbis Outline. PAGE 56: Courtesy of House of Cash. PAGE 57-58: Les Leverett Collection. PAGE 60, TOP: Courtesy of Tara Cash Schwoebel. PAGE 60, BOTTOM: Les Leverett Collection. PAGE 61: ©Jim Marshall. PAGES 62-63: Colin Escott/Michael Ochs Archives. PAGE 65: Courtesy of David Fricke. PAGES 66-67: Colin Escott/Showtime Archives, Toronto. PAGE 69: Robert Spencer/Retna. PAGE 73: AP Photo. PAGE 75: Michael Rougier/Time Life Pictures/Getty Images. PAGE 77: London Features International. PAGE 79: The Everett Collection. PAGE 81: The Everett Collection. PAGES 82-83: Hulton/Archive/Getty Images. PAGE 85: Michael Rougier/Time Life Pictures/Getty Images. PAGE 86: Photofest. PAGE 87: Courtesy of Mississippi Valley Colection/University of Memphis Libraries. PAGE 88: Photofest. PAGE 89: J.T. Phillips/Globe Photos. PAGE 90: Ken Regan/Camera 5. PAGE 91: Gene Bealy/AP Photo. PAGES 92-93: ©Jim Marshall. PAGE 94: Alan Messer/Star File. PAGE 95: Rick Diamond/Wire Image. PAGES 96-97: ©Jim Marshall. PAGES 100-101: ©Jim Marshall. PAGE 103: Photofest. PAGES 105-131: Courtesy of Cindy Cash, Tara Cash Schwoebel, Kathy Cash Tittle and Rosanne Cash. PAGE 133: Alan Messer/Star File. PAGE 137: Mark Seliger/Corbis Outline. PAGES 138-139: Adam Scull/Globe Photos. PAGE 140: Michael Ochs Archives. PAGE 143: Courtesy of Rosanne Cash. PAGES 144-149: Kevin Estrada/Retna. PAGE 154: Peter McDiarmid/Camera Press/Retna. PAGE 155, TOP: Larry Busacca/Retna. PAGE 157: Mark Seliger/Corbis Outline. PAGE 159: Courtesy of Rosanne Cash. PAGE 162: Danny Clinch/Corbis Outline. PAGES 164-165: Courtesy of Rosanne Cash. PAGE 166: John Chiasson/Getty Images. PAGE 169: Martin Schoeller/Corbis Outline. PAGE 171: Annie Leibovitz/Courtesy of Rosanne Cash. PAGE 173: Christopher Little/Corbis. PAGES 174-176: Courtesy of John Carter Cash. PAGE 177: Bettmann/Corbis. PAGE 179: Mario Geo/*Toronto Star*/Zuma Press. PAGE 181: Michael Rougier/Time Life Pictures/Getty Images. PAGE 185: Dick Friske/Globe Photos. PAGE 186: Les Leverett Collection. PAGE 195: David McClister. PAGES 196-198: The Everett Collection. PAGE 200: Bettmann/Corbis. PAGE 201, TOP: NBC/The Everett Collection. PAGE 201, BOTTOM: CBS/The Everett Collection. PAGE 202: The Everett Collection. PAGE 203, TOP: Hulton/Archive/Getty Images. PAGE 203, BOTTOM: The Everett Collection. PAGE 205: Luciano Viti/Retna. PAGE 206: Globe Photos. PAGE 207: Henny Garfunkel/Retna. PAGE 208: Kevin Mazur/Wire Image. PAGE 209: Mark Seliger/Corbis Outline. PAGE 210: Alan Messer/Rex Features. PAGE 211: Michel Arnaud/Corbis Outline. PAGE 212: Len Irish/Corbis Outline. PAGE 213: Mark Arbeit/Corbis Outline. PAGE 214: Steve Granitz/Wire Image. PAGE 215: Linda Matlow/Pix International/Wire Image. PAGE 216: Steve Granitz/Wire Image. PAGE 217: Dana Tynan/Corbis Outline. PAGES 218-219: Hulton/Archive/Getty Images. PAGES 220-221: Alan Messer/Star File. ENDPAPER: Danny Clinch/Corbis Outline.

I love songs about horses, railroads, land, Judgment Day, family, hard times, whiskey, courtship, marriage, adultery, separation, murder, war, prison, rambling, damnation, home, salvation, death, pride, humor, piety, rebellion, patriotism, larceny, determination, tragedy, rowdiness, heartbreak and love. And Mother. And God.

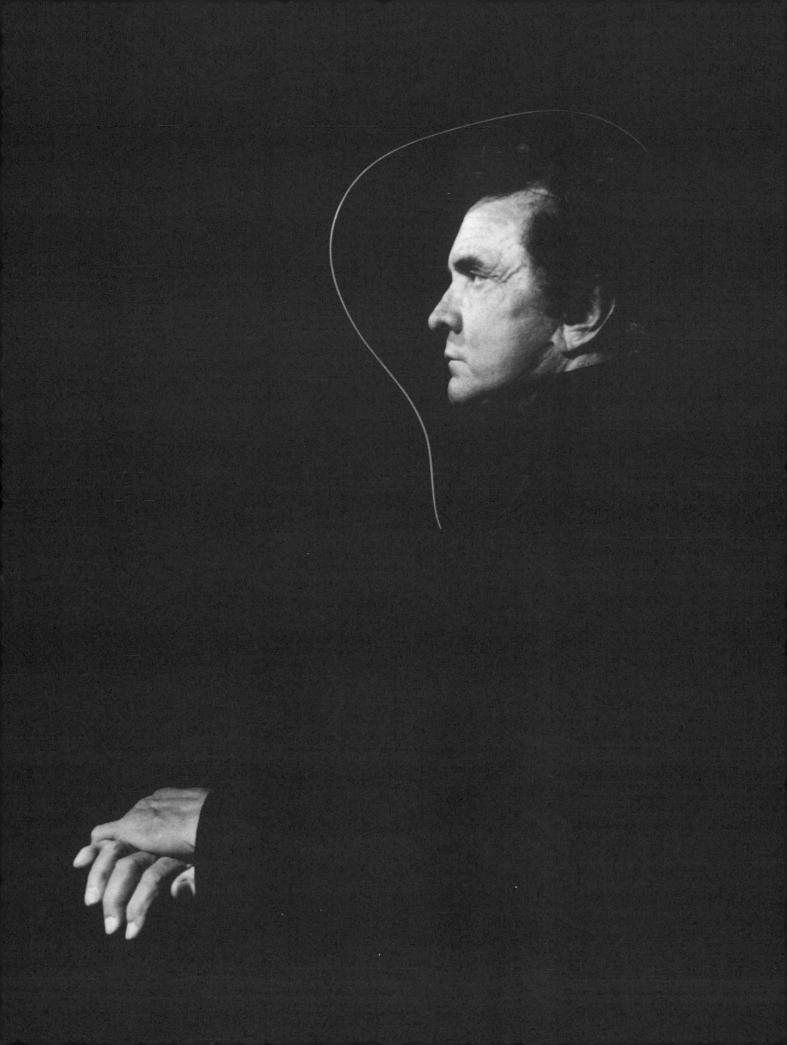

B
CASH        Cash.